THE COUGAR

Look for these and other books in the
Lucent Endangered Animals and Habitats Series:

The Amazon Rain Forest
The Bald Eagle
The Bear
Birds of Prey
The Cheetah
Coral Reefs
The Elephant
The Giant Panda
The Gorilla
The Jaguar
The Manatee
The Oceans
The Orangutan
The Rhinoceros
Seals and Sea Lions
The Shark
The Snake
The Tiger
Turtles and Tortoises
The Whale
The Wolf

Other related titles in the Lucent Overview series:

Acid Rain
Endangered Species
Energy Alternatives
Environmental Groups
Garbage
Hazardous Waste
Ocean Pollution
Oil Spills
Ozone
Population
Saving the American Wilderness
Zoos

THE COUGAR

BY NATHAN AASENG

Endangered
Animals &
Habitats

LUCENT BOOKS, INC.
SAN DIEGO, CALIFORNIA

Library of Congress Cataloging-in-Publication Data

Aaseng, Nathan.
  The cougar / by Nathan Aaseng.
      p. cm. — (Endangered animals & habitats)
Includes bibliographical references and index.
  ISBN 1-56006-730-6 (hardcover : alk. paper)
  1. Pumas—Juvenile literature. 2. Endangered species—Juvenile litera-
ture. [1. Pumas. 2. Endangered species.] I. Title. II. Series.
  QL737.C23 A15 2001
  333.95'97524'0973—dc21

                                                            00-009796

Contents

Introduction

PREDATOR. THE NAME has an ominous ring to it. Predators represent the most savage element of nature. They are the killers who seek out unwary or helpless creatures to attack and eat.

Humans have always been both attracted to and repelled by nature's predators. Part of the fascination lies in the appreciation of the sheer strength of these beasts. Indeed, the larger the predator, the greater the emotions it inspires. The long-extinct tyrannosaurus remains a subject of endless wonder far beyond that of smaller and less formidable extinct creatures. Along with brute strength, large predators carry the allure of danger. In a world that humans have tamed, shaped, civilized, and sterilized to their own whims and needs, the free-roaming predator stirs up the human sense of adventure and challenge.

At the same time, the power and danger associated with large predators have made them mortal enemies of the human race. Particularly in the culture that emerged from the Europeans who settled in North America, predators have been targeted for destruction in an effort to rid the land of their menacing presence.

Conflict between humans and predators has left the United States with only five species of large predators: the grizzly bear, black bear, gray wolf, jaguar, and cougar. Grizzly bears occupy only a few isolated federal lands. Except for small populations in a few northern states, wolves have been pushed out of the country. Jaguars only rarely appear on the very southern fringe of the country. That leaves the black bear and the cougar as the only predators still surviving in significant numbers.

Of the two, the cougar is by far the more formidable hunter. Whereas the black bear can depend on plants for a large portion of its diet, the cougar is, pure and simple, a meat eater. The cougar is programmed by nature to kill and eat virtually any living creature that it comes across. It is equipped with a variety of weapons that make it the most accomplished and efficient hunter of all the large land creatures. The cougar is the only predator that regularly hunts and kills—single-handedly—animals that are more than five times its size. One researcher found that Idaho cougars who have singled out a victim succeed in bringing down their prey eight out of ten times. In comparison, the lightning-quick cheetahs achieved success about one out of every two hunts, the mighty lion one out of ten, and the tiger fewer than one out of ten.

People marvel at the imposing strength and size of predators such as the long-extinct tyrannosaurus.

The cougar's unmatched combination of speed, agility, and strength make it a formidable hunter, capable of killing animals five times its size.

Nowhere else in the natural world can such a combination of speed, strength, and agility be found. Martin Jalkotzy experienced the speed of the big cats while tracking a cougar through the snow near Banff, Alberta. "I was walking around my millionth spruce of the day, when all of a sudden a cougar exploded from underneath it. I know it was a cougar, yet it moved so fast that I have no image in my mind of that cat. It was gone before my eyes could focus."[1]

The cougar's feats of strength and agility are no less astounding. The force of its charge can put a one-thousand-pound bull moose on its back. Cougars have been known to drag a six-hundred-pound elk up a mountain in their jaws. They can leap more than thirty feet in a single bound and maneuver down cliffs that would challenge a mountain goat.

Yet this marvel of creation has drawn nothing but contempt from people throughout most of the past three centuries. Theodore Roosevelt derided the cougar as the "sneak cat,"[2] hunters sneered at it as a coward, and ranchers lumped it with rats and mice as vermin. Many of them believed that the extinction of the cougar would be a blessing to the world.

That point of view has fallen from favor in recent years. A large number of people have come to agree with nineteenth-century philosopher Henry David Thoreau, who wrote, "When I consider that the noble animals have been exterminated here—the cougar, panther, lynx, wolverine, wolf, bear, moose, deer, the beaver, the turkey—I cannot but feel as if I lived in a tamed and . . . emasculated country."[3]

One does not need to see a cougar in the wild to benefit from its existence. Indeed, the cougar moves with such stealth that even most outdoor enthusiasts have never laid eyes on one except in zoos. But many of those who hike the mountains and deserts of western North America realize that cougars have probably seen them. Just knowing that these magnificent ghosts of the wilderness are still out there, doing what nature has equipped them to do for thousands of years, feeds the spirits of those in tune with the natural world.

Furthermore, modern science has taught that predators are not cowardly villains that destroy the gentler animals of creation. Rather, they are an important part of a complex web of interactions between animals and plants. Humans have finally come to understand that the balance of nature is delicate and that tampering with that balance is dangerous. Removing a key link such as the cougar runs the risk of ecological catastrophe.

1

Decline of the Cougar

TRACING THE ORIGINS of the cougar is a project that has baffled even the best fossil detectives in the world. The basic structural design of cats has proved so marvelously adapted to their meat-eating style of life that it has changed little over the centuries, even though the species have diverged greatly in their outward appearance. As Kevin Seymour, vertebrate paleontologist at the Royal Ontario Museum in Toronto, notes, "If a cougar and a jaguar walked into a room, you'd have no trouble telling them apart. But just try to distinguish them from their bones!"[4]

The fossil record shows that small tree-dwelling, insect-eating animals with many of the characteristics of today's mammals appeared on earth about 65 million years ago. About 20 million years later, this animal gave rise to two families of carnivores, the felines (cat family) and the canines (dog family). When the dinosaurs died out, huge saber-toothed cats emerged as the dominant predators in the Western Hemisphere.

Cougars' rise to the top

Exactly where the cougar fits in to the evolutionary tree remains something of a mystery. An early cat known as *Felis daggetti* appears to be the forerunner of the small cat family, in which biologists included cougars, ocelots, and wildcats. More recently, evidence has suggested that the modern species of cougar is also related to the cheetah of the Eastern Hemisphere, which was long thought to occupy its own separate branch of evolution.

Some experts believe that a longer-legged version of the cougar first appeared from 1 to 3 million years ago and that the modern cougar eventually branched off from it as recently as 100,000—possibly even 30,000—years ago. Others argue that the cougar species has existed in basically its present form for at least 3 million years and possibly for as long as 8 million years. Either way, the cougar or its ancestor lived in the shadow of the fearsome saber-toothed cats and huge American lions. But when these giant predators disappeared following the last advance of the great glaciers into what is now the United States, about ten thousand years ago, the cougar suddenly took over as the dominant cat on the continent.

Cat of many names

The cougar proved to be a master of adaptation. It went on to make itself at home virtually everywhere in the Western Hemisphere, from the Canadian Yukon to the Strait of Magellan at the extreme southern tip of South America. Cougars prowled the snowy forests of Canada, where the temperatures

A man holds up the skull of a saber-toothed cat. These fearsome animals were dominant predators until their extinction about ten thousand years ago.

What's in a Name?

The confusion over the common English name of the largest American cat continues even to this day. British biologists argue that the animal is properly called the puma, yet that name is seldom used in the United States. Among the sixteen states in which the animal is acknowledged to live, eight state wildlife management agencies refer to it as the cougar, seven as the mountain lion, and one as the panther.

Common names for the largest American cat are cougar, mountain lion, and puma.

fall well below 50 degrees Fahrenheit, and the sweltering rain forests of Central America. They could be found in the barren deserts of the southwestern United States and in the humid swamps of the Everglades in Florida, at sea level along both the Pacific and Atlantic coasts, and at more than fifteen thousand feet in the Andes Mountains.

The animal's common names reflect this wide distribution. The cougar is listed in the dictionary under more names than any other animal in the world. There are at least forty-two accepted names for the animal in the English language alone, with hundreds more in Spanish and the various dialects of native peoples.

The name *puma* came from a word that meant "powerful animal" in the Quechua language of South American mountain-dwelling peoples. Natives of the Amazon region of South America called the animal *cuguacuarana*, which means "false deer." In the eighteenth century, the influential French biologist Georges Buffon adopted a shortened form of this name, *cougar*, as the common name for the beast.

The explorer Amerigo Vespucci and his crew were the first Europeans to see a cougar. While sailing off the coast of Nicaragua in 1500, they observed an animal that appeared to be identical to the female lion of Africa. In their reports, they identified the animal as *leon,* or lion. Spanish explorers, believing that all the specimens they saw were females and that the males were extraordinarily secretive and elusive, continued to use the term for the animal. When encroaching civilization eventually pushed these animals into the more remote and less inhabited mountain regions, the big cat became known as the mountain lion.

Various locales developed their own names for the cougar. Those in the southern United States began to refer to it as a *panther.* Backwoodsmen such as legendary rifleman Davy Crockett put their own variation on this, referring to the beast as a *painter.* New Englanders often spoke of the "cat of the mountains," which was eventually shortened to *catamount.*

Swedish biologist Carl Linnaeus dubbed the cougar Felis concolor, *a Latin name meaning "cat of one color."*

Cat of one color

To clear up some of the confusion caused by its multiple common names, the eighteenth-century Swedish biologist Carl Linnaeus devised a system of Latin names to distinguish each species of living things. He named the cougar *Felis concolor*, or "cat of one color." The name refers to the fact that, unlike many larger cats, the cougar has no spots or stripes. But descriptions of cougars prove that the name is misleading. There are two distinct color patterns among cougars, light brown and gray, and even within these patterns large variations exist. Cougars have been described as red, brown, buff, cinnamon, tawny, silver, and gray. In addition to their dominant color, their ears and the tip of their tail are nearly black, and their underbellies tend to be white.

Linnaeus lumped the cougar in with the small cats in the genus *Felis*, as opposed to the large cats, the *Panthera*. He did so partly because cougars lack the hyoid bone at the root of the tongue, the bone responsible for the distinctive roar of the large cats. Like their smaller cousins, cougars can purr and hiss, and they can snarl and even emit a loud, haunting scream, but they cannot roar. In addition, cougars share behaviors of smaller cats such as grooming themselves by licking their fur with their tongues, sharpening their claws on rocks or trees, and crouching when they feed.

But again, the classification is not perfect. Some cougars, for example, are larger and heavier than some of the large cats such as leopards and jaguars. In addition, some of their bone structure appears to be more similar to the cheetah, which has been put in its own genus, than to small cats. In recognition of this, in 1993, many biologists put the cougar in its own separate genus and called it *Puma concolor*.

Although cougars can emit an intimidating snarl, they cannot roar.

Are all cougars the same?

The cougar is a long, low, muscular animal with a small, rounded head, a short face, and a fairly long neck. The cougar's tail, which is longer and thicker than that of larger cats, may be half as long as the rest of its body. The average male grows to about seven feet in length and weighs just over 140 pounds, although some have tipped the scales at well over two hundred pounds. Females tend to be about 20 percent smaller than males. Cougars have powerful shoulders and their forelegs are shorter and more muscular than their long, leaner hind legs. This gives them an appearance that experts have described as something like a cheetah on a weight-lifting program.

Cougars in dry mountainous regions, such as this cougar from Colorado, tend to be larger than other cougars.

Like all animals, cougars have had to adapt to an ever-changing environment in order to survive. These adaptations include slight differences in appearance among cougars living in different parts of the Western Hemisphere. For example, cougars in the dry mountainous regions of Utah, Arizona, and Colorado tend to be slightly larger than others, while cougars of Central America run a little smaller than the average.

The minor variations have led to a great deal of confusion as to whether they are characteristic of an entire group or just variations among individuals. In 1901, an *Outdoor Life* magazine article claimed that cougars and mountain lions were different species. In the 1940s, scientists described a separate subspecies of cougar called *Felis concolor couguar*, based on eight specimens found in New York, Pennsylvania, and Virginia. In recent years, some specialists in animal classification have divided cougars into as many as thirty subspecies.

The quibbling over subtle differences among cougars may seem like a trivial matter, but it is important in terms of endangered animals. If, for example, there are thirty distinct types of cougars and one of these types begins to die out, that type could be an endangered subspecies. Wildlife advocates would then take urgent measures to protect it. On the other hand, if all cougars in the United States are basically the same, then dwindling numbers of cougars in one location would not necessarily be a cause for alarm.

Decline of the cougar

There is no way of knowing how many cougars roamed the Western Hemisphere in centuries past. But they appear to have been the dominant predator on the American continents for several thousand years. Since virtually all Native American peoples were familiar with them, it is safe to assume that cougars were common in the centuries during which they shared their range with Native Americans.

When Europeans began probing the Americas in the late fifteenth century, the cougar population was large enough so that, even though the animals are secretive and experts at staying out of sight, many explorers observed them without having to move inland from the coast. In fact, the big cats were such a constant presence all along eastern Canada to Florida that colonists considered them a nuisance.

Cougars did not coexist well with the European settlers who came in ever growing numbers to settle in the New World. As large population centers were established on the east coast of what became the United States and pioneers pushed westward to carve farmlands out of the wilderness, cougars retreated into the uninhabited lands. As a result, cougar populations in all eastern states steadily dwindled. By 1850, cougar sightings were rare in the eastern United States, occurring mostly in the rugged mountains and forests where few people lived.

One by one, the eastern states rid themselves of the last remaining cougars. The last confirmed cougar in Vermont was killed in 1881. Cougars disappeared from a previous stronghold in the southern Appalachians in the 1920s. Maine recorded its last known cougar kill in 1938. That left the eastern United States with only a small population holding out in the inaccessible Florida wilderness.

The story of cougars disappearing before the advance of civilization repeated itself throughout their range. A once-thriving population of cougars in Central America melted away as the human population grew. The cougar range in South America shrank steadily. Cougars were driven out of Minnesota, Louisiana, and the Ozark Mountains of Missouri and Arkansas in the early 1900s. At about the same time, intensive government cougar-control programs reduced cougar populations to precariously low levels throughout the western United States. Even California, which had been home to the largest cougar population of all the states, saw its numbers decline to around six hundred in 1920.

Endangered or thriving?

The stealth and secrecy of the cougar makes accurate cougar population numbers extremely difficult to obtain. But all the evidence points to the big cats making a remarkable comeback in the last half of the twentieth century. U.S. National Parks Service biologists estimated in 1965 that somewhere between 7,300 and 17,500 cougars remained in North America. About 4,000 to 6,000 of those lived in the United States, with the rest in western Canada.

The population of the Florida panther, the most endangered cougar, has dwindled to between thirty and fifty individuals.

Recent estimates put the North American figures at somewhere between 20,000 and 35,000, with the great majority of those living in the western United States. There are now significant numbers of cougars in eleven western states, plus Texas and South Dakota. California's cougar population rebounded to nearly 2,000 by 1972, and has since expanded to roughly 5,000. Other cougar strongholds in the United States include Oregon and Arizona, with 3,000 each, and Idaho, with 2,000. British Columbia remains the prime cougar habitat in Canada, with an estimated 3,800 cats, including nearly 800 on Vancouver Island alone. Alberta is home to at least 700.

In most of these areas, the cougar populations appear to be stable and, in some cases, growing. Arizona and Colorado are believed to have more cougars than they

had a decade or two ago. Texas has experienced an increase in the number of reports of cougar sightings, including sightings in central Texas, where the animal had not been reported for many years. Experts caution that reported cougar sightings are a highly inaccurate gauge of the animal's population. Wildlife professionals who follow up on reported cougar sightings have found that, in a majority of cases, the animal sighted was not a cougar. Nonetheless, the cougar population in western North America appears to be thriving.

The most seriously threatened cougar population resides in Florida. The *Puma concolor coryi*'s numbers have been so devastated that only thirty to fifty individuals are believed to survive. The cougar populations of Costa Rica, Panama, Honduras, and Nicaragua have also been decimated; thus the animal's survival is at risk in those Central American countries as well. Despite an almost total lack of accurate scientific information about South America's cougar popu-

 Was There Ever an Eastern Subspecies?

A debate has raged among biologists and wildlife enthusiasts as to whether the cougars that once thrived in eastern North America were a distinct subspecies that has since disappeared. For a time, a majority of biologists accepted the existence of *Felis concolor couguar*, the eastern cougar. But in 1994, Melanie Culver, a researcher at the Laboratory of Genetic Diversity in Frederick, Maryland, performed tests that cast doubt on the validity of that assumption. Culver's DNA testing of cougars from a wide variety of locations in the Western Hemisphere suggested that all cougars in North America were virtually the same, with the exception of the Florida panther. A report from the government-sponsored Committee on the Status of Endangered Wildlife in Canada concluded from this that the eastern cougar may never have existed as a subspecies and that, rather than being exterminated, it was merely driven into the western part of its range.

lation, experts believe the species has been steadily declining throughout the continent.

Ghost of the eastern woods

The most controversial debate over cougar populations centers on eastern North America. Although the cougar has been declared extinct throughout this region, there has been some evidence that a few cougars may roam the land. Spotty signs of this have been trickling in for more than thirty years. In December 1976, five park rangers at the Great Smoky Mountain National Park in eastern Tennessee witnessed a cougar chasing a deer. A few months later, experts confirmed that a deer carcass had been the victim of a cougar kill. Evidence of a cougar presence kept coming until the park superintendent in 1977 declared, "It is apparent that mountain lions once again live in the Smoky Mountains."[5] In subsequent years, a few cougars were killed in the backwoods of West Virginia and Tennessee. Authorities, however, believed that none of this was the result of a wild cougar population but rather that the cougars were pets that had been released after the owners discovered how much trouble they were to keep.

New evidence indicates that cougars, once declared extinct throughout eastern North America, may be living in the Smoky Mountains (pictured) in eastern Tennessee.

For many years, cougar sightings and evidence such as hair and feces have been reported in New Brunswick, Canada. Biologist Bruce Wright kept a detailed documentation of a cougar population that most experts insisted did not exist in that province. During the 1990s, mounting evidence convinced many outdoorsmen in the area that cougar populations were living secretly in the forests. Ted Reed of Nova Scotia saw a cougar run along the side of a road and then clear it in a single leap. The experience led Reed and others like him to gather hundreds of pieces of evidence of cougar sightings in eastern Canada, Maine, Vermont, New Hampshire, and even western Connecticut.

Government officials such as Steve Parron of Vermont's Agency of Natural Resources noted, "The sightings that

20

have been reported to me usually have some sort of detail that doesn't quite match up."[6] But some pieces of evidence were hard to dispute. One cougar was captured by a video camera in New Brunswick; another was photographed in Maine.

In November 1992, game officials positively identified tracks and hair found in New Brunswick as belonging to a cougar. Three years later, experts in the Portland, Maine, area confirmed that a patch of fur found in the woods belonged to a cougar, and a Vermont Fish and Wildlife Service biologist identified droppings in that state as a cougar's. In March 1996, game wardens near Cape Elizabeth, Maine, found cougar tracks in the snow and cougar hair.

Indisputable evidence of cougars came in from other places where cougars were believed to be extinct. Conservation officials in Minnesota treed and captured a female cougar in 1991. A videotape of a cougar in southern Missouri in 1996 was found to be authentic, as were cougar hair and droppings.

Skeptics such as Ted Reed doubted the standard official line that the cougars involved were animals that had escaped from captivity or been released by unhappy owners. He found it unlikely that a captive animal whose claws had been removed, who lacked experience in the wild, and who had never had to learn hunting skills could survive in the wild. "This is an animal that has never become extinct in the northeast, even though the government authorities insist it has,"[7] Reed declared.

Melanie Culver's research at the Laboratory of Genetic Diversity in Frederick, Maryland, however, offered evidence that the authorities were correct. Her test of the DNA of one of the eastern cougars showed that it probably came from Chile. The DNA testing caused Don McAlpine, curator of the zoo at the New Brunswick Museum, to change his mind about the probability of a remnant cougar population surviving in the east. "My feeling is that there are not any eastern cougars left,"[8] McAlpine said in 1999.

It remains a mystery exactly where these occasional ghosts of the eastern forests came from—whether they are escapees from zoos or released pets or wanderers from populations far to the west. However, most biologists currently doubt that there are any viable breeding cougar populations in eastern North America.

Cougar status

Contrary to the beliefs of some nature enthusiasts, the cougar, as a species, is in no immediate danger of extinction. This does not, however, mean that its existence can be taken for granted. The immediate danger is that certain cougar populations, including subspecies such as the Florida panther, may be lost forever. Just as the once-abundant cougars of eastern North America were lost, Florida, Central America, and regions of South America are in grave danger of losing their cougars.

Furthermore, there are trends in human behavior that will make it difficult even for the thriving cougar populations of western North America to survive in the future.

2

Life of a Wild Cougar

ENSURING THE SURVIVAL of the cougar in its various habitats requires an understanding of exactly how the animal lives and what it requires for its existence. The elusive cougar has yielded its secrets sparingly over the years, but wildlife biologists have gained at least some understanding of how it interacts with its environment.

Physical adaptations

The cougar is one of the most perfectly designed all-purpose predators on dry land. With a body made up largely of muscle, it has physical capabilities far beyond those of any other North American predator. In the words of naturalist Ernest Thompson Seton, the cougar's "daily routine is made of stirring athletic events."[9] It has stocky, powerful forelegs capable of delivering a knockout blow with a single swipe. Its paws are lined with one-inch, razor-sharp claws that can hook on to prey or split open its skin. Cougars are equipped with the short cat muzzle and extremely powerful jaws. Their jaws and neck are so strong that the cats have been known to drag seven-hundred-pound animals for hundreds of yards. The four one-and-one-half- inch incisors in those jaws provide a lethal bite that can sever a spinal cord or rip open a throat.

The cougar's hind legs and its back are long and slim, providing the animal with superb leaping and sprinting ability. Cougar leaps have measured at nearly forty feet on flat surfaces, and its vertical jumps of up to eighteen feet allow it to spring up steep rock faces. One cougar was reported to have jumped twelve feet up a rock ledge carrying a one-hundred-pound buck in its jaws. Those same hind legs provide the power that launches the cougar from a crouching position into a terrifying missile. Combined with its lightning reflexes, this explosive charge allows it to burst from a hidden position almost more quickly than the human eye can detect. Few people have seen a cougar in full sprint, but experts estimate that it can run at speeds of nearly forty-five miles per hour for a short period of time. Like all cats, cougars have relatively small hearts, which prevent them from sprinting for more than a few hundred yards before becoming exhausted.

The cougar has far more going for it than power and speed. Like all cats, it moves silently over all types of ground. Padding about on soft paws, it is able to retract its sharp claws so that they do not hit the ground. The earth-tone colors of the cougar also help it to blend in well with many types of natural surroundings.

Powered by their long, slim, and muscular hind legs, cougars can leap great distances.

Cougars are also incredibly nimble creatures. Because they are so adept at climbing up and down steep rock faces, they are the only land predator capable of going after bighorn sheep and rocky mountain goats in high mountain ranges. One research team trying to track cougars in Idaho was continually frustrated by the animals' agility. The crew had to spend an entire white-knuckled afternoon inching down sheer cliff faces to follow a cougar that nonchalantly bounded down the cliffs in a few seconds. Cougars can also swim well, but they almost never enter water unless they absolutely must.

Other cougar attributes include excellent vision, from which it gains most of its information about its surroundings, and acute hearing. Cougars also have the ability to tolerate greater extremes in weather conditions than virtually any other animal in the world. Even those cougars that live in the harshest environments require no specialized shelter; they may find temporary shelter in caves or thick vegetation but generally lie down in any moderately protected area when they need to rest.

Preferred habitat

Because they are so well equipped for hunting and are adaptable to different climates, cougars can operate in a wide variety of habitats. The animal seems to require little for its existence beyond the availability of prey, the presence of ground cover, and a wide territory to roam.

Cougars require ground cover because, despite their arsenal of lethal weapons, they have a great deal of trouble catching prey that can see them coming. Their limited circulatory and respiratory systems do not allow them to chase prey for great distances and so they must depend on their ambush skills to acquire food. They thrive best in the cover of forests and in mountainous areas where they can hide among the rocks. Yet cougars have also been able to survive in flat, barren areas because their coats blend in well with the surrounding land.

The only habitats in North America where cougars have not been able to establish themselves are in areas where

large concentrations of humans do not tolerate their presence, in regions where humans have eliminated cougar prey, and in the extreme north. The inhibiting factor in northern Canada is not the cold but the tree line. In the treeless tundra, cougars have nowhere to hide among the short stubby vegetation, and their tawny coats stand out in the snow that covers the land for half the year.

The stealthy cougar hides behind ground cover in order to ambush its prey.

Territoriality

Like most cats, the cougar is a loner. Each individual establishes its own hunting territory and is very protective of that territory. That territory is never less than five square miles even in the best cougar habitat, and is more often in excess of twenty square miles. Females require less territory, from five to twenty-five square miles, while males stake out ranges of fifteen to thirty square miles. One Texas cougar was found to patrol a home territory of nearly seven hundred square miles. Cougars, who generally travel from one to five miles a day in their search for food, may take a week or more to complete a circuit of their territory. The territory may vary from season to season, especially in areas where the cougars' prey migrates. The summer territory is generally larger than the winter range.

In typical cat fashion, cougars mark the limits of their territory with urine to alert other cougars that this area is already taken. There can, however, be some overlap in ranges, especially between males and females. The territory of one male cougar was discovered to overlap the territories of eight females, a behavior that increases the male's mating opportunities.

The cougar population within any given area is constantly changing. Cougars with established ranges die, leaving their territories vacant, while young cougars coming of age are looking to claim territory of their own. Cougars have been tracked over distances of five hundred miles as they wander in search of unclaimed territory. In highly populated cougar areas, some cougars may never establish a territory of their own and will have difficulty surviving.

There is some disagreement among experts over the nature and frequency of territorial disputes. Some argue that cougars show great respect for another cougar's established territory and that fights between cougars are rare. "Male cougars are usually quite careful to avoid encroaching upon the marked home range of another male cougar," according to cougar expert Harold Danz, "but when this does occur, the subordinate male most often will retreat."[10]

Other experts argue that brief spats over territory are fairly common, even among females, but that injuries in such cases are rare. Yet other researchers have found territorial fights to be a major cause of death among cougars. In the late 1980s, one male in the San Andreas Mountains of New Mexico killed three females whose ranges bordered his.

The probable reason for the discrepancy in opinion is that, although avoidance of other cougars is a trait of all cougars, aggressiveness varies widely according to the individual. Some cougars simply are prone to fighting while others avoid it.

Reproduction

Female cougars are capable of breeding at about two-and-a-half years of age. They generally produce a litter every other year until they are about twelve.

Most animals who live in cold weather climates avoid mating at times when a pregnancy would result in a midwinter birth because their babies would have difficulty surviving the harsh weather. Contrary to popular belief, however, cougars have no specific breeding season. Researchers in Alberta have found that cougars are as likely to have kittens (because cougars were considered members of the small cat group, their offspring are called kittens, whereas large cat offspring are called cubs) in midwinter as in any other time of year, and those kittens are as likely to survive as kittens born in milder seasons. In fact, experts believe there may be advantages to midwinter births: Predators such as bears are asleep during the winter, the eagles have migrated, and prey are easier to catch because they are weaker from hunger and because they have difficulty running in deep snow.

Cougar kittens, unlike other animal offspring, are often born in midwinter and have the ability to survive harsh winters.

Since males and females avoid each other most of the year, the female must advertise when she is ready to mate. She does this through chemicals in her urine, with which she marks her territory, and by a loud mating scream.

A mating couple will stay together for only a week or two. During this time, they may mate fifty to seventy times a week. When the mating period is over, the cougars part. Males have no role in providing for their offspring; in fact, they will eat the kittens if they find them unprotected.

A cougar pregnancy lasts from ninety to ninety-six days. The litter size can be anywhere from one to six kittens, with two or three being the most common. Cougar kittens are identical to snow leopard cubs at birth. But the dark spots on the body and the dark streaks on the tail begin to fade by two months. They are barely visible at eight months and disappear altogether by one year.

Raising the young

Cougar mothers protect their kittens by hiding them in shelters such as caves or rocky crevices.

Cougar kittens are tiny and helpless at birth. They weigh from eight ounces to one pound and are not able to open their eyes for the first ten days. Although adult cougars require no shelter, the females must provide a nest for their offspring. This can be anything from a cave or rocky crevice to a secluded spot screened by thick underbrush. The mother is careful to keep the area concealed and as neat and clean as possible.

For the first five or six weeks, the kittens stay in the nest, gaining their nourishment through nursing. Gradually, the kittens switch their diet to meat, supplemented by insects and berries. The mother may have to leave the nest for up to thirty hours as she searches for food. This leaves the kittens, who are often in open-air nests even in the most bitterly cold climates, exposed to the elements and predators. During the mother's absences, the kittens huddle together to keep warm.

When the kittens become stronger, the mother may carry them to her kills. Eventually, they can follow the mother on their own. The mother keeps them from wandering astray by calling them with chirplike whistles.

As the kittens grow older, the hunting burden becomes extremely stressful to the mother. Normally, a lone cougar can survive by killing an animal such as a deer every ten days to two weeks. But a female cougar with two or three large youngsters may have to bring down a deer every three days in order to satisfy everyone. A researcher in Idaho discovered one ninety-four-pound female who was still providing all the food for three kittens, each of which was larger than she. In such a situation, cougar mothers cannot afford to waste any meat. They typically sleep within a few yards of their latest kill to prevent other animals from scavenging the meat.

Littermates usually get along very well. Young cougars spend much of their time at play, during which they develop the skills they will need for ambushing and killing prey. One California female was observed bringing live grasshoppers for her month-old kittens to practice catching. The kittens frequently stalk and pounce on their mother's long tail and wrestle with each other.

At anywhere from fourteen to twenty-four months, the kittens leave the mother. Many times this departure occurs when the young cougars are driven off by their mother's new mating partner. Littermates often stay together for two or three months after leaving the mother, then separate and go off in search of their hunting territories.

Cougar diet

Cats are the most specialized meat eaters of all the land predators. Unlike bears and even canines, they seldom eat anything but meat. In fact, their simple digestive systems are unsuited to anything else.

Cougars have voracious appetites and, to satisfy them with the least expenditure of energy, they prefer large animals. Their main food source in any habitat, as long as it is available, is deer. The whitetail deer of North America is the

Deer are the favorite prey of cougars because they are not intimidating and thrive in areas open to ambush.

perfect size for the cougar's needs. With an average weight of 160 to 300 pounds, it can provide a cougar with sustenance for a week or two. Although the deer is a fast runner, it usually thrives in areas where a cougar can hide and ambush it, and it is normally not large enough to pose a danger to a healthy cougar.

When cougars are not able to find deer, they will settle for virtually any other animal they come across. One detailed California study of a cougar over the course of a year found that it killed forty-eight deer and a wide selection of fifty-eight smaller animals to fill in during lean times.

The size of the prey is seldom a concern to a hungry cougar. In areas where larger antlered animals such as elk and deer predominate, cougars will focus on these animals as their primary prey. Not even a thousand-pound bull elk or moose is safe from a cougar attack. The big cats are such efficient killers that they do not necessarily follow the general predatory rule of focusing their efforts on young, very old, weak, or sick prey. Since such prey is easier to catch, cougars probably will target them if they have a choice and will have more success catching them than they do healthy animals. But cougars are opportunistic hunters who will take the first unwary creature they come across, regardless of its age or condition. An Idaho study found that only about half their victims were in poor condition.

 A Dangerous Way to Make a Living

Although American frontiersmen often derided the cougar as a coward, the animal is one of the few predators in nature that regularly risks its life to get a meal. Almost all other predators attack prey that is smaller and far weaker than they are, but cougars will not hesitate to go after some formidable targets, and under hazardous conditions. Bull moose and elk are enormously strong animals that can use their superior size over the cougar to good advantage. They, as well as deer, mountain goats, and bighorn sheep, can defend themselves well with sharp hooves and antlers when attacked.

In one documented incident, a cougar was killed when an elk trying to shake loose from it flung the cougar into a sharp branch. Another cougar attack ended when the mule deer on which she had pounced careened down a steep slope and slammed into a pine tree, breaking the cougar's back. Yet another cougar met its end going after a bighorn sheep on a steep mountain face. Both the cougar and the sheep lost their footing in the struggle and fell ninety feet to their deaths.

Even a slight injury in an encounter with its prey can prove disastrous to a cougar. A cougar hobbled by injury has little chance of bringing down a large prey or matching the quickness of smaller prey and so could starve before the injury heals.

Bighorn sheep can use their large horns to thwart a cougar attack.

Cougars are opportunistic hunters that will occasionally chase smaller prey such as rabbits.

A cougar's craving for fresh meat is so great that it will kill and eat any living creature it encounters with no apparent regard for taste. Cougars have been documented eating mice, rabbits, squirrels, opossums, porcupines, raccoons, beavers, bobcats, foxes, mountain goats, armadillos, alligators, turtles, frogs, turkeys, ducks, grouse, and fish. A hungry cougar is one of the few animals that will endure the horrible stench of a skunk in order to eat it.

Since hungry cougars will not turn up their noses at any live prey, they pose a danger to both humans and domestic animals that they encounter in their territory. In past years, cougar attacks on domestic animals were almost exclusively aimed at livestock. Cougars are especially attracted to horse meat and will take abnormal risks to get it. But recently, as suburban developments have pushed into cougar habitat, cougars have found pets such as dogs and cats to be irresistible snacks.

Master of the ambush

Ever flexible in their quest for meat, cougars will hunt either by day or by night, depending on the habits of their prey. They tend to be more active by day in areas where there is no regular human presence.

Cougars are effective stalkers because they move silently, hide well, and show amazing patience. A cougar will stand motionless for half a day waiting for prey to wander within striking distance. Cougars try to approach their main prey, deer, from behind. Once they draw within thirty feet, their explosive charge can usually close the distance before the deer has time to accelerate to top speed. If the initial attack does not succeed, the cougar makes no attempt to chase the deer. It will pursue only slower animals.

Cougars kill small animals with a single blow from a paw. For larger animals, they attempt to knock over the beast by slamming into it high on the shoulder or neck. Holding the fallen animal down with their front claws, they then dispatch their prey with a bite at the back of the neck or base of the skull that severs the spinal cord. On the rare occasions when this fails to do the job, they sink their teeth into the victim's throat. Only seldom do they have to resort to strangling the prey by clamping down on the windpipe. Cougars have been known to kill very large elk by jumping on the back, reaching down with a powerful front paw, and pulling the neck back, breaking it.

After the kill

The cougar usually drags its victim to a secluded place immediately following the kill. There the short-winded animal can take time to recover from the strenuous effort of the attack. They then gorge themselves on their kills—consuming up to eighteen pounds of meat at a feeding. After eating their fill, they cover the remains with a mound of debris known as a "scratch hill" to discourage scavengers.

A cougar will return to feed on the carcass a number of times as long as the meat remains reasonably fresh, which can be up to two weeks in cold weather and much less in warmer weather.

Cougars' strong preference for fresh blood makes them wasteful eaters. Even though ample meat remains from a kill, they will continue to hunt, returning only if they are unable to capture new prey. Seemingly programmed by nature to kill whenever the opportunity presents itself, cougars can be ruthless killers that slaughter every animal

A cougar kitten has a 90 percent chance of surviving into adulthood as long as it is protected by its mother.

within reach. One rancher reported that a cougar who broke in to an enclosed sheep pen killed 192 of the animals in a single night.

Natural threats to existence

An adult cougar has little to fear from predators, although there have been instances in which wolves and bears competing for habitat have killed big cats. The kittens are more vulnerable to predation from wolves, bears, and eagles. But they grow quickly and, under the protection of the mother, appear to have a high survival rate. As long as the mother is alive, experts believe that cougar kittens may have as much as a 90 percent chance of surviving to adulthood.

Captive cougars have lived as long as twenty-five years. The life span of cougars in the wild, however, is about eight to eleven years. The most common natural causes of adult cougar death are starvation, injury and accident, territorial combat, and disease. During the past couple of centuries, however, the main threat to cougars has not come from the natural world. It has come from humans.

3

Cougars Versus Humans: Hunting

COUGARS AND HUMANS have been encroaching on each other's territory for probably forty thousand years. Some people, such as German zoologist Bernhard Grzimek, believe that it has always been an uneasy, if not hostile, relationship. "Since ancient days," says Grzimek, "people have hunted carnivores with a hostility bordering on madness. . . . To kill a carnivore, wherever it could be found, was unreservedly viewed as a creditable deed."[11]

Native americans and cougars

Such a sweeping statement, however, reflects a rather narrow cultural view. The relationship between cougars

Some Native Americans such as the Hopi admired the cougar and believed that it was a sacred animal. Modern Hopi are shown here performing a tribal ceremony.

35

and the Native Americans with which they shared the land for many centuries was not as antagonistic.

The Indian tribes that spread throughout two continents varied greatly in lifestyle and customs, and their attitudes toward the cougar varied accordingly. Some, such as the Hopi of what is now the southwestern United States, admired the cougar and viewed it as a somewhat sacred animal. Although they recognized that the beasts needed to be treated with caution, some Native Americans considered cougars to be friends and allies. When Jesuit missionaries in California during the sixteenth century tried to enlist the aid of local Indians to kill cougars as a means of protecting livestock, the Indians refused. Even when the missionaries offered them a bull for every cougar killed, they found no takers. The cougar, said the Indians, was their friend. They remembered lean times in their past when they had been able to survive only by scavenging meat from cougar kills. Native Americans in South America told a legend about a cougar that protected a helpless girl caught in the rain forest at night from approaching predators. Other Native American attitudes ranged from simple acceptance to fear. According to Harold Danz, the one common thread in Indian attitudes toward cougars was that they all treated the animal with respect and accepted it as a part of their world.

Many tribes hunted cougars for food, and some prized their claws as a decoration for necklaces. But cougars were not a primary source of food, or an especially targeted quarry, for any Indian group. Although they were skilled trackers and hunters, there is no evidence that Native Americans ever killed cougars in numbers that significantly affected their population.

War on the species

The European explorers and pioneers who arrived in increasing numbers in the Americas had an entirely different attitude, one more in line with Grzimek's reflection. In their view of civilization, everything in the environment existed to benefit the needs of humankind. Nature was a chaotic force to be tamed or eradicated as much as possible if it could not be made to serve those needs.

When they arrived in the Americas, European pioneers found themselves in constant battle with nature. Their style of living depended on clearing land for agriculture and bringing in and raising domestic animals that were not native to the area. These animals were unable to defend themselves against the wild predators that roamed the perimeters of the small clearings that the settlers had carved out of the wilderness. For poor settlers whose wealth was tied up in only a few cows, the loss of one to an opportunistic cougar was a tragic blow. For a pioneer family depending on deer meat to get them through the winter, the sight of a potential meal killed and eaten by cougars was infuriating. Therefore, early pioneers and settlers viewed the abundance of cougars and other large predators as a major problem.

In the words of wildlife writer Ted Williams, "Quickly, Europeans set about trying to rectify this fact by declaring war on the species, behavior that flabbergasted the Indians and for which their only explanation was that whites were insane."[12]

The life of a European pioneer in America depended on clearing land for agriculture and raising domestic animals.

Predator slaughter

The first pioneers dealt with cougars and other predators on an individual basis. Initially, they simply killed these animals on sight. Then they tried trapping and poisoning, followed by hunting. Eventually, they joined forces with other colonists in an attempt to eliminate such animals from their domain once and for all.

The most extreme example of this war of annihilation was the animal drive. Settlers began the drive by completely clearing a large section of land. Then they fanned out from this clearing until they ringed a vast circle of land some thirty miles in diameter. All the settlers would then set fires and make as much noise as they could around the perimeter of the circle. Still lighting fires and making a racket, they advanced through the woods toward the center of the circle, driving all animals within it before them. When the settlers closed the circle, the animals would all be trapped without cover in the central clearing, where the settlers slaughtered them.

In one documented animal drive in 1760 near the eastern seacoast, the colonists killed more than 1,000 animals, including 41 cougars, 109 wolves, 112 foxes, 114 bobcats, 17 bears, and 12 wolverines. They disposed of most of the animals by simply burning them. Indian outrage over such waste contributed to conflicts between them and the colonists.

The colonists eventually abandoned their brutal animal drives, turning instead to professional hunters and the government for aid in their war against predators. One of the first examples of government intervention was a 1695 law in South Carolina that required all Indians in the state to kill a cougar, bear, wolf, or two bobcats each year or be subject to a public flogging. At about the same time, Connecticut put into practice the policy of bounty hunting. Under the bounty system, the government paid a set amount for every animal killed. All of the other original thirteen colonies joined Connecticut in offering cash bounties for the destruction of all large predators.

Easy kills

American pioneers singled out cougars as special targets for elimination because of their utter disdain for the big cats. They labeled cougars as "vermin" or "varmints"—utterly worthless pests in the same vein as disease-carrying rats. Ascribing human characteristics to wild animals, they considered cougars to be vicious, bad-hearted beasts with no redeeming qualities whatsoever. Frontier settlers were especially disdainful of what they considered cowardice in the cougar. In 1709, North Carolina historian John Lawson observed that "the least cur [inferior dog] could chase a cougar into a tree."[13]

Western pioneers and hunters held the grizzly bear in great respect because of its size, fearlessness, and difficulty to kill, yet spoke of the cougar with scorn. They derided the cougar

Cougars use their climbing skills to escape from wolves (pictured) and other predators that possess superior stamina.

as a bully that preyed on helpless animals but could not put up any kind of a fight when challenged by a real adversary. This attitude would continue well into the twentieth century.

In fact, cougars proved to be surprisingly easy to kill, thanks to a combination of two tools of hunting that the Indians had not employed. The first of these was the gun. The cougar is primarily a mass of muscle. It lacks the massive skeleton of an animal such as a bear and, as a result, cougars can be easily killed with small-caliber guns.

The second tool was the hunting dog. Since cougars are short-range sprinters that tire quickly, they have no hope of outrunning attackers that have more stamina, such as wolf packs. Over the centuries, cougars responded to this danger by developing an escape strategy. When pursued by wolves, they made use of their superior climbing skills by seeking refuge in trees. Since wolves cannot climb, the cougars merely had to wait in the tree, for days if necessary, until the wolves lost interest.

Cougars, particularly in rugged terrain, could usually elude hunters tracking them without dogs. They had little to fear from dogs by themselves—cougars have felt so safe in their high refuges that they have been known to fall asleep while dogs frantically jumped and barked beneath them. However, the ancient strategy of tree climbing was of no use when dogs and humans joined forces. Hunters could follow the dogs unhurriedly and pick off the treed cougar at long range with a gun. Suddenly, cougars found themselves facing a determined enemy that had both the will and the means to kill them in large numbers.

Professional cougar hunters

As the population expanded westward, cougars in western states drew the wrath of farmers and ranchers, who despised the big cats for occasionally taking their livestock. Every state among the lower forty-eight, with the exception of Nevada, eventually put a generous bounty on cougars. The state of Oregon, which initiated its cougar bounty in 1843, offered $50 per dead cougar, a considerable sum in those days. It was tempting enough to attract the best hunters in the land, some of whom made a career of killing cougars.

One of the most famous of the professional cougar hunters was Ben Lilly. An Alabama-born backwoodsman who liked to hunt alone with his specially trained pack of dogs, Lilly hunted cougars with religious fervor during the late 1800s and early 1900s. He firmly believed that he was rendering a great service to the world by ridding it of an evil species. During his long hunting career, he estimated that he killed more than six hundred cougars, including nine in a single week.

Farmers and ranchers were not the only people who called for the services of the professional hunter. Sport hunters and even some early conservationists believed that cougars had to be eliminated to promote the health of preferred game such as deer. Aiming to protect deer and elk herds, park employees and visitors shot cougars on sight in Yellowstone National Park at the turn of the twentieth century. In the summer of 1905, cougar hunters systematically eliminated all remaining cougars from the park, killing at least sixty-five of them.

At about the same time, the federal government established a natural game preserve on the Kaibab Plateau of northern Arizona. By "natural game," the government meant nonpredatory animals only. Federal officials approved a drive to guarantee the safety of animals such as mule deer by

Elk at Yellowstone began to overgraze their range when efforts were made to eliminate cougars from the park at the turn of the twentieth century.

eliminating cougars from the Kaibab. Within twenty-five years, nearly eight hundred cougars and virtually all other predators were killed in the game preserve. James Owens, a former game warden, led the onslaught, personally killing more than six hundred of them on the plateau.

Both the Yellowstone and Kaibab programs produced exactly the opposite effect of what was intended. Free from cougar predation, elk at Yellowstone overgrazed their range, damaging vegetation and driving out deer herds. Since there were no longer any cougars on the Kaibab, the mule deer population soared from around 4,000 to more than 100,000. This was far more deer than the habitat could sustain. The result was widespread deer starvation and destruction of vegetation. Nonetheless, many game experts continued to view cougar killing as a necessary game conservation measure.

Headed for extinction

Unlike their more colorful cousins, such as leopards, tigers, and ocelots, the plain-coated cougars were not hunted for their furs. But, ironically, even though most outdoorsmen considered cougars cowardly and easy to kill, the big cats did fall victim to trophy hunters who wanted a cougar skin as evidence of their daring and expertise in overcoming a powerful beast. These amateur hunters, among whom Theodore Roosevelt was the most prominent, hired professional guides to find and tree cougars for them to shoot. The seven Lee brothers from Tucson, Arizona, made a living as cougar-hunting guides for more than sixty years. During that time, they estimated that they and their clients hunted down more than one thousand of the animals.

Protective farmers and ranchers, bounty hunters, government predator-control programs, and trophy hunters combined to devastate the cougar populations not only in North America but in Central and South America as well. At one point, it appeared that the species was headed toward extinction. In California, home of the largest cougar population in the United States, the animal was hunted down to an estimated six hundred individuals by 1920.

Amateur hunters such as former president Theodore Roosevelt (pictured) hired professional guides to find and tree cougars.

Uneasy truce

By retreating to inaccessible wilderness areas, the cougar population managed to hold out until its archenemy experienced a change in attitude. By the middle of the twentieth century, the public started to become concerned about the elimination of wild animal species from the world. Trophy hunting was no longer viewed as proof of manliness but, rather, as the senseless slaughter of a valuable resource.

Conservation studies also helped turn the tide against widespread hunting of cougars. Ecologists were able to educate the public about the importance of predators in maintaining a balanced ecosystem. People learned that, far from destroying valued animals such as elk and deer, cougars helped to keep those populations at a sustainable limit.

By the mid-1960s, all western states and provinces stopped paying a bounty for cougars.

For a brief time, some of them continued to allow the indiscriminate killing of cougars. But eventually, with the single exception of Texas, where any cougar could be shot on sight at any time, all of them declared the animal a big game species and set up regulations and limits on hunting it. As a result, cougar numbers began to rebound. Within a decade of ending its bounty in the early 1960s, California's cougar population bounced back to about two thousand.

The once-despised Florida panther has been designated as the state animal of Florida.

Modern bans on cougar hunting

As the environmental and animal rights movements grew stronger, the cougar gained more dedicated and influential friends. The state government of Florida designated the once-despised Florida panther as its state animal. In 1972, California lawmakers banned all cougar hunting except in cases in which a cougar presented an immediate danger. Within a few years, the government of Chile passed a similar law.

Not everyone, however, embraced the movement to protect cougars. In 1980, California governor George Deukmejian

Cougars have occasionally attacked lone mountain bikers, who probably appear to be fleeing prey to the predators.

announced that he would veto any legislative attempt to extend the cougar-hunting ban. This led cougar advocates to mount an intensive campaign to put the issue before the people. In 1990, California voters passed Proposition 117, which not only banned the sport-hunting of cougars but also authorized the government to spend $30 million a year in acquiring and preserving cougar habitat.

Four years later, the state of Oregon, where more than six thousand cougars were killed by bounty hunters between 1843 and 1967, passed Measure 18 which banned hound hunting of cougars. That same year, the Colorado Wildlife Commission closed the cougar-hunting season from March 31 to November 1 on the assumption that these were the months when females and their new kittens were most susceptible and that a seasonal ban would allow them to grow up.

The cougar issue returned to California elections in 1996. This time, despite a spirited effort by opponents of the cougar-hunting ban, California voters rejected Proposition 197, which would have returned to the State Department of Fish and Game the option of setting up cougar-hunting regulations as a means of controlling the big cats' population. South Dakota and Florida, which have very small cougar populations, have joined California in prohibiting cougar hunting.

Cougars versus humans

The controversy over controlling cougar populations is fueled by the fact that the conflict between humans and cougars is not completely one sided. Unlike many dangerous wild animals, cougars will attack humans without being provoked. Although humans are never the normal, preferred prey of cougars, cougars are opportunistic predators. When they are hungry, they will go after any living creature that comes within reach, including humans.

Children make especially inviting targets because cougars can sense their inability to defend themselves. Lone joggers and mountain bikers also attract the interest of cougars, probably because they appear to be prey that are trying to flee. A person kneeling to drink at a stream also presents an irresistible image of unwary prey.

The first recorded incident of a fatal cougar attack occurred in Pennsylvania in 1751. The legendary frontiersman Kit Carson was among many who told the tale of being badly injured by a cougar attack in the nineteenth century. For most of the twentieth century, however, cougar attacks were rare. In the past century there have been only fifteen documented fatalities caused by cougars and fifty nonfatal attacks.

Growing concern

Despite these figures, cougar attacks have been a growing concern on the west coast of the United States, for two reasons. First, the frequency of the attacks has been increasing in recent years. No cougar attacks on humans were reported in California between 1910 and 1986, but since then, four fatal attacks and at least nine other attacks have occurred. Those who favor cougar hunting argue that this is a result of overpopulation caused by the hunting ban. They believe that unhunted cougars are becoming

Surviving a Wilderness Encounter with a Cougar

As increasing numbers of people enter cougar habitat while hiking or exploring the wilderness, the potential for a cougar encounter grows. The odds of a person meeting a cougar in the woods or mountains remains extremely remote. Those odds can be reduced even further with a few precautions:

1. Never hike, jog, or bike alone in an area where cougars are known to exist. Cougars are far more likely to approach a lone person than groups of two, three, or more.

2. Small children should never be allowed to wander off. The majority of recent cougar attacks have been against children. Like all predators, cougars are especially attracted to prey they can easily catch and kill, and an unguarded child makes a tempting target.

Cougars are often curious about humans and will follow them for a while to satisfy their curiosity. However, they can do this without being seen. In rare cases when a cougar appears and does not immediately run off, the cougar should be carefully studied for clues about its intentions. A cougar whose eyes are intensely focused on a person poses a serious threat. Other signs of immediate danger are a quivering tail, dropping into a crouch, and ears laid flat or halfway back against the head. When these signs are present, the following rules should be observed.

1. If a safe place, such as a car or house, is near, take refuge there immediately, but . . .

2. Do not run away. This can trigger an immediate attack response from a predator that is used to chasing fleeing prey.

3. Do not approach the cougar.

4. Do not turn away. Stare the cougar directly in the eyes and do not break eye contact.

5. Raise your arms to try and make yourself appear bigger than you are. Do not bend over except to quickly grab a club or stone. Lift small children off the ground.

6. If the cougar approaches, shout and wave your arms. If the animal attacks, fight back with whatever weapon is available. Do not play dead or be submissive, as the cougar's intent is to make a kill to eat and lack of resistance only makes its work easier. Protect your face and neck as well as possible.

more aggressive and fearless and are expanding into populated areas. Incidents such as a cougar padding through a crowded campground in California with a coyote in its mouth in the 1990s lend support to this view.

Cougar ban proponents, however, note that more than half the cougar attacks in past decades have occurred on Vancouver Island in Canada, where cougar hunting has always been legal. They argue that aggressive cougars tend to be inexperienced youngsters looking to establish a territory. Such cougars who pose a danger to humans do not live long. "Since cougars tend to be more reclusive, whenever and wherever an unprovoked attack on a human takes place, it is considered an extraordinary event, and swift action is taken to destroy the animal,"[14] says Harold Danz.

A second cause of concern over cougar attacks is that when the animals attack, they do so with the intention of eating the victim. The image of a person being consumed by a large cat is too gruesome for most people to contemplate. Therefore, when a fifty-six-year-old woman was ambushed and killed by a mountain lion in Cuyamaca Rancho State Park in southern California, and a high school distance runner was attacked and eaten while training in Colorado, both in the mid-1990s, the emotional response of the public was great. Cries for the control of the cougar population were a predictable result.

Wildlife advocates counter that there is an irrational bias against cougars that magnifies cougar attacks far out of proportion. For example, roughly fifty herdsmen are gored to death by cattle each year, and this is considered an unfortunate occupational hazard. The death of one person a year to cougar attack, however, prompts demands for action against cougars. At least forty people die each year in the United States from bee stings, yet bee population control is not an issue. Furthermore, a person is 650 times more likely to be killed by lightning than to be killed by a cougar. Nonetheless, pressure persists to continue or revert to the policies of predator control that have killed an estimated eighty thousand North American cougars in the twentieth century alone.

4

Cougars Versus Humans: Habitat Loss

ALTHOUGH INTENSIVE HUNTING has decimated cougar populations and driven them from much of their former range, cougars today are threatened much more by habitat loss than by the barrel of a gun. According to Bernhard Grzimek, "The greatest and currently still-growing threat [to wildlife] is the geometric progression in the destruction of habitats."[15] Danz makes the case more specific when he says, "Habitat loss is the primary cause of the cougar's uncertain future."[16]

Habitat loss is an indirect, often unintentional, threat to wildlife. There are no skins on the wall testifying to the cougar destruction, only the slow, steady retreat of animals into ever smaller and more remote areas. The amount of available habitat for cougars has shrunk relentlessly over the years—sometimes gradually, sometimes dramatically—and is continuing to shrink.

Early cougar habitat destruction

As devastating as the campaigns of annihilation against the cougar have been, habitat and prey loss have been even more of a factor than hunting in this animal's disappearance from the eastern United States. In the centuries before the arrival of European settlers, cougars had free access to virtually all the land. The lifestyle of the Native Americans did not require the removal of cougars or alter the habitat so that it was unsuitable for the animals.

The European colonists and pioneers, however, brought with them a lifestyle that was incompatible with the needs of wild animals. The settlers claimed the most fertile valleys for themselves and then set about changing the environment to suit their needs. The first order of business was to clear the land for farms, and in so doing they destroyed cougar habitat, one small section at a time.

Making room for domestic animals

More devastating yet was the settlers' dependence on domestic animals to support their lifestyle. Not only did the settlers have to clear land for grazing, but they had to take steps to protect their flocks and herds from wild animal predation. In addition to hunting, the settlers cleared far more forest land than they actually needed in order to deprive predators, such as cougars, of the cover they needed to stalk domestic animals.

By 1820, the vast forests that had covered New England were largely destroyed. The effect of this combined with intensive hunting devastated the wild animal populations. The formerly plentiful white-tailed deer was all but eliminated from the northeastern United States. Unable to find deer on which to feed, cougars died out, moved away, or

The European settlers' intensive hunting coupled with their destruction of vast forests resulted in the near elimination of white-tailed deer (pictured) in the northeastern United States.

attempted to feed on the only available food source—
domestic animals, which only accelerated eradication
efforts against the few cougars that remained.

The story was repeated, county by county, as the American settlers moved west. Prior to 1790, there were an estimated 110,000 European settlers living west of the Appalachian Mountains and east of the Mississippi River. Even considering the settlers' destructive effects on the environment, this still left considerable habitat for cougars. But in the next twenty years, a flood of settlers moved west, swelling the population of the region to more than 1 million. As on the east coast, the combined effect of so many people living a lifestyle incompatible with the existing land eliminated much of the wilderness and the animals that had lived in it.

The population continued to grow and expand all the way to the west coast over the next century. Everywhere people went, they cut forests, plowed under the prairies to plant crops, and fenced in range land for their herds and flocks. Cougars had to retreat to ever more remote and inhospitable lands. By the middle of the twentieth century, the cougar had been pushed out of nearly two-thirds of its former range.

Reverence for land versus competition for resources

At about this time, people in the United States finally woke up to the effects of unregulated habitat destruction. U.S. Secretary of the Interior Stewart Udall summed up the change of attitude in 1963 when he said,

> In recent decades we have slowly come back to some of the truths that the Indians knew from the beginning: that unborn generations have a claim on the land equal to our own; that men need to learn from nature, to keep an ear to the earth, and to replenish their spirits in frequent contacts with animals and wild land. And most important . . . we are recovering a sense of reverence for the land.[17]

This newfound emphasis on environmental awareness, however, could not by itself solve the problem of habitat

Mining is one of several industries aggressively seeking to expand into wilderness habitats and national parks.

loss. The expanding population of the United States has grown used to a certain standard of living that continues to make large demands on natural resources. Thus, inevitable collisions of interest between the habitat needs of cougars and the habitat needs and wants of human society persist.

The competition between humans and wildlife for every remaining habitat is stiff. Cougar experts trace the animal's decline in Central America to the destruction of habitat resulting from the region's rapidly growing human population. Wilderness habitats, even national parks, are under constant pressure from real estate agents whose clients want to live in a natural setting, from consumers whose energy and water requirements lead to damming rivers, and from industries looking to mine precious metals and harvest valuable timber.

Habitat fragmentation

Conservationists have been successful in getting the government to set aside certain tracts of federal land as wilderness areas. Many of these areas seem as though they would be large enough to sustain a small population of cougars. "As long as we don't cover all their territory with houses and shopping malls, they'll still be out there,"[18] writes Ted Williams.

But the fact is that small populations do not reproduce well. Mating animals with very similar genetic information tend to become inbred, producing less vigorous and less fertile offspring than those produced by couples with different genetic information. Wildlife researchers working in New Mexico concluded from their studies that a breeding population of 250 adult cougars of each sex is needed for the genetic variation that will ensure the survival of the species for at least a hundred years. Studies have also shown that each cougar requires a great deal of territory in which to hunt for the food it needs. The healthy minimum population of five hundred cougars would require ten thousand square miles of continuous habitat in order to survive. Such continuous habitat is scarce and growing scarcer.

When their habitat is fragmented, cougars trying to establish new territories frequently find themselves in unfamiliar and dangerous areas. Cougars attempting to cross highways that separate sections of their habitat often end up dead. One researcher of roadkill in the Cuyamaca Rancho State Park area near San Diego, California, recorded eighteen cougar fatalities within a ten-year period.

Cougars are frequently hit by cars when attempting to cross highways that separate segments of their habitat.

The fragmentation of habitat also forces cougars to stray outside of their preferred territory and into more populated areas. Ray Lee of the Arizona Department of Game and Fish comments, "Predators start having an impact [on human lifestyles] when you have severe habitat fragmentation. We're seeing that pretty much everywhere with the highways, water development, [and] mines."[19]

Pressure points-overlapping habitats

As the human population continues to grow, the human desire for developing wilderness resources increases, and conflicts between cougar interests and human interests grow ever more acute.

"It's overwhelmingly popular to have these animals in our ecosystem," notes Tom Dougherty of the National Wildlife Federation. "But if they're in your backyard, some people aren't loving it."[20]

The fact is that more and more backyards are bumping into the cougar habitat in both North and South America. Some blame cougars for this. The editors of *Field & Stream* magazine say the mountain lion population "has clearly overgrown its natural range and is expanding into urban areas, often with tragic results."[21] The small increase in cougar numbers, however, is a drop in the bucket compared with the increase in the human population. Many observers blame human expansion for the increase in cougar attacks in recent years. Given that cougars are predators designed to kill any living thing that comes within range, most experts believe that there is simply no way that cougars and humans can share the same habitat. Therefore, any expansion of humans into the wilderness results in the elimination of cougars. Says Ted Williams, "The best way to avoid confrontations with lions is to give them the space they need."[22]

California is a prime example of the problems that erupt when an expanding human population encroaches on cougar territory. Within the past forty years, California's population has more than tripled, making it by far the most populous of the United States. Much of that population has

Upsetting Complex and Fragile Ecosystems

In recent years, scientists have found that interrelationships between all forms of life within a particular habitat are incredibly complex. Small changes in the habitat can have far-reaching and unforeseen consequences, and the solutions are rarely as simple as they seem. California's bighorn sheep population provides a case in point.

Bighorn sheep have been clinging precariously to existence in the eastern Sierra Nevadas of that state. In the late 1990s, Dr. John Wehausen, who was studying bighorn sheep at the White Mountain Research Station, raised a warning that the sheep were on the verge of extinction. Its numbers had dropped from an estimated three hundred to near one hundred. The culprit, according to Wehausen, was California's growing cougar population. In response, the federal government in April 2000 declared the Sierra Nevada bighorn sheep endangered, which allowed officials to take aggressive actions against cougars to protect the sheep.

California's cougar numbers had nearly tripled since the ban on cougar hunting had been put in place in the early 1970s. The fact that the cats were now wiping out the bighorn sheep led many to the logical conclusion that the hunting ban had allowed cougars to overpopulate the mountains and had put the sheep at risk. These people advocated reinstating a cougar-hunting season to thin cougar numbers and save the sheep.

The truth proved to be a great deal more complex. Vern Blaisch, a senior wildlife official with the California Fish and Game Department, said that, contrary to popular belief, cougar numbers were not soaring out of control. The hunting ban had simply allowed the cougar population to return to its former level, a level at which bighorn sheep in the past had never been in danger. Although it was true that cougars posed a present danger to the sheep, that was because the ecosystem had been thrown out of balance by other factors. The sheep population had declined to extremely low levels not because of cougars but because of decades of overhunting and severe habitat loss.

Had the habitat been more carefully preserved, according to experts, the sheep population would have been able to thrive despite cougar predation. "Changes that would go unnoticed in a more resilient population can wipe out a species that's in trouble," noted Vern Blaisch in "Looking for Bighorns in All the Wrong Places?" an article published by *Field & Stream*. As proof of that, biologists pointed to Arizona's bighorn sheep population. With far more suitable habitat, Arizona's sheep population held steady at around six thousand despite the presence of a large cougar population.

In any case, experts noted that opening up cougars to hunting would be of little value to California's sheep. Sport-hunting, they observed, was not a fine-tuned-enough system to be able to weed out those few cougars that had targeted sheep as a primary prey.

sprawled out from urban centers into former wilderness areas, putting housing developments on the edge of cougar habitat. Cougars living in these adjacent areas have recently come to associate humans with food, especially where their habitat has been so fragmented that it can no longer provide them with adequate wild prey. Young cougars looking to establish a range of their own have little choice but to explore the fringes of these suburban developments.

It is not humans themselves on which cougars learn to prey but, rather, their pets. Dogs and cats make easy meals for cougars. Unfortunately for cougars, people are even more emotionally attached to pets than they are to domestic animals. The killing of a pet provokes outrage and demands for the removal of the cougars, even though it was human encroachment that created the problem.

Furthermore, a pet that is killed in a yard brings home the fact that these dangerous animals are uncomfortably close. A cougar intent on attacking a pet displays a single-mindedness that overrides its normal avoidance of people.

Many suburban developments, some of which encroach on cougar habitat, have been constructed to accommodate California's sprawling population.

In one example, a cougar chased a dog through an open door into a living room. Cougars that openly display themselves in suburban areas are viewed as menaces that need to be eliminated.

Harmful effects of "getting back to nature"

Ironically, the public's renewed interest in the natural world has made life more difficult for cougars. For increasing numbers of people, the ideal home is one nestled on the edge of wilderness country, away from the congestion and noise of the city. They enjoy the unspoiled land and the chance to see occasional wildlife.

Most such people, however, also take their modern habitat-altering culture with them to the wilderness. They bring creature comforts such as roads, cars, and electric power lines. After a few homes move into an area, that area becomes attractive to people looking for a suburban setting that is free from city problems. These people bring with them necessities such as schools and churches and conveniences such as shopping centers. As the community becomes more settled, those who originally built there to live among nature become irritated. They move out farther to the new edge of the wilderness and the cycle of suburban development is repeated, gobbling up more expanses of wilderness habitat.

Nature enthusiasts have also taken to remote hiking and biking trails in growing numbers. Because many of the most unspoiled areas are in the middle of prime cougar habitat, this brings increasing numbers of people into contact with cougars. Cougar attacks become more frequent, bringing calls for the removal or elimination of the beasts.

The Florida panther: Case study in habitat loss

Critics of those who advocate protective measures for cougars point out that the cougar

The endangered Florida panther, a cougar subspecies, is slightly darker than most cougars, has longer legs, and a broad, flat nose.

is not presently an endangered species. It continues to thrive in many locations, and its numbers, at least in North America, have increased over the past several decades. There are, however, cougar subspecies and populations that are endangered, largely because of habitat loss. The most critical of these is the *Cougar concolor coryi*, a distinct subspecies of cougar more commonly known as the Florida panther.

The Florida panther is slightly darker than most cougars, has longer legs, and has a broad, flat nose. A few centuries ago, an estimated two thousand to thirty-four hundred Florida panthers roamed the southeastern United States from Florida to Texas and as far north as Tennessee. In the nineteenth century, as the rest of the cougar populations in the east were wiped out, the Florida panther survived by retreating into the inaccessible swamplands of Florida.

Much of the Florida panther's habitat was destroyed during the development that followed the construction of Disney World.

Make way for humans

With the nearest cougars far to the west in Texas, the panther became isolated from all other cougar populations. This was not a problem as long as the Florida panthers enjoyed enough habitat to support a large population. But in the twentieth century, even the remote wetlands of Florida came under the bulldozers of civilization. Much of the wetlands were drained and turned into cattle ranches or orange groves. This was followed by a massive influx of people. Retirees, attracted by Florida's warm climate, poured into the state. Walt Disney built a popular amusement park in the center of Florida that attracted millions of tourists and businesses seeking to serve those tourists. The small city of Orlando, home to only 30,000 residents in 1965, swelled to more than 250,000 within a decade, and soon topped 1.5 million. As the hordes moved in, rural wetlands were drained to make way for housing subdivisions.

Florida's population explosion resulted in the construction of highways that pass through and fragment the Florida panther's habitat.

The human population explosion had a domino effect on many factors affecting cougars, all of them bad. Habitat destruction devastated the deer populations on which panthers depended for their survival. In order to service the streams of traffic caused by the population boom, Florida constructed three major interstate arteries. These highways broke the Florida panther's remaining habitat into small pieces. The panthers tried to maintain their territories by crossing highways when necessary, with disastrous results. Highway kill became a significant cause of death among the animals.

Poisoning caused by pesticides used in agriculture added to the panthers' woes. In past centuries, pioneers had found it almost impossible to poison cougars. Since cougars have a strong preference for fresh meat, they were not attracted to poisoned carcasses. But in the twentieth century, accidental poisoning targeted the panther more than many other animals. Prey animals ingested poisonous substances such as mercury in amounts too small to harm them. But as the cougars ate these animals, they absorbed the poisons of each prey until the accumulated amounts became lethal.

Researchers discovered that raccoons were the primary cause of mercury poisoning in panthers. Had the panthers been able to prey on deer, such contamination would not have affected them much. But in the absence of deer, they were feeding heavily on raccoons, with ominous results. According to a Florida legislature subcommittee report, "Chronic exposure of Florida panthers to mercury appears to be compromising their relative health and possible productivity; especially in the Everglades portion of the ranges; mercury must be considered a threat to their continued existence."[23]

Past the point of no return

As a result of habitat loss and other factors, Florida panthers have nearly been exterminated. They have been forced into the deep swamps that are as yet too unappealing for humans to develop. Although cougars are among the most adaptable animals on earth, not even they find these swamps hospitable. Prey is scarce and harmful parasites abound.

No one knows exactly how many Florida panthers remain in these wetlands. Those that remain are almost impossible to find. Naturalist Ted Levin once spent three weeks tracking the Florida panther. Although he used the best equipment and most experienced trackers, he never saw a single panther. Most experts estimate, however, that no more than thirty to fifty adults remain.

That is grim news for the panthers since experts say that five hundred breeding adults are needed to maintain a healthy population. Decades of inbreeding among the few panthers has already taken its toll. Researchers have found that 94 percent of Florida panther sperm is abnormal, which leads to reproductive failure and immune system collapse. A study by Melody Roelke of twenty-three Florida panther pregnancies found that only ten kittens were able to survive beyond six months.

Worse yet, there is no indication that Florida will ever be able to support a thriving population of panthers. Even if no further development were to take place—an unlikely proposition—the state does not have enough remaining habitat to support the necessary five hundred animals to maintain healthy genetic diversity. Only thirty-five hundred square miles of habitat remain, half of that on private land that can be developed at any time should the owner so choose. According to the experts, this habitat is not capable of sustaining much more than fifty adult cougars.

5

Trying to Understand Cougars

ATTEMPTS TO DETERMINE the cougar's chances of future survival have been hampered by a shortage of information. Cougars are among the most secretive large animals on earth. They avoid contact except when they initiate it. They move silently, hide well, and prefer habitat in which transportation is difficult. Many nature lovers have spent a lifetime hiking through wilderness areas that are home to cougars without ever seeing one.

Mysterious animals

This secrecy means that, although cougars can be tracked, treed, and killed fairly easily by hunters with dogs, they have been extremely difficult to study. Even some scientists who study cougars have never seen one except those treed, killed, or trapped. One author spoke to a hundred of the world's top cougar experts yet was unable to find one who had actually seen a cougar making a kill. There is virtually no documented information about issues crucial to the species' survival, such as how many kittens in a litter survive to adulthood.

Wildlife authorities have found that it is difficult to determine a cougar's age and almost impossible to count the number of cougars in a given location. The big cats move so quickly that glimpses of them are usually fleeting, and the desire to see these formidable creatures in the wild often influences a person's perception. Such a large percentage of

Cougars move so quickly that glimpses of them are usually fleeting.

reported cougar sightings have turned out to be false that experts dismiss such reports as "worthless or worse as an indicator of cougar presence, cougar numbers, or trends in cougar numbers."[24]

The lack of verifiable information on cougars means that much of what people have believed about cougars has been based on guesswork or just plain prejudice. According to one veteran cougar researcher, "Those who had worked with lions for only a few years were convinced they knew what makes the big cats tick; those who had studied cougars over ten years felt they were just beginning to scratch the surface."[25]

Mistaken conservation policies

Government and organizational policies have been based on (and continue to be based on) these mistaken beliefs, and as a result they have sometimes done more harm than good. The policies of predator annihilation put in place in the early twentieth century were not simply the product of uneducated, stubborn individuals. They were based on opinions of some of the most active and well-read conservationists of the day.

One of the most basic conservation philosophies of 1900 was that killing bad animals was necessary to save the good animals. This concept of predators as "bad" was not simply a superstition or a character judgment. Even wildlife experts of the time thought of predators as basically oversized germs that wreaked havoc on helpless animal populations wherever they turned up.

In 1913, William T. Harnady, director of the respected New York Zoological Society, gave a speech to forestry students at Yale University in which he stated, "The eradication of the puma from certain districts that it now infests to a deplorable extent is a task of immediate urgency. . . . At this moment, pumas are a curse to the deer, elk, and other game."[26]

M. P. Skinner, a wildlife researcher who studied Yellowstone National Park in the 1920s, expressed a similar view. Cougars, he said, "are the deer slayers, and we find we must keep their numbers down if we would preserve any of the deer."[27] Jay C. Bruce, a predator-control specialist for the state of California in the 1920s and '30s, declared that cougars were worthless animals that cost the state thousands of dollars every year in meat alone.

The Hornocker studies

During the twentieth century, strong evidence emerged that killing off cougars was not the best way to manage wildlife. In many states where predators such as the cougar were eliminated or their numbers greatly reduced, deer populations grew out of control. But, because of the difficulties in studying cougars, there was no hard evidence of the ways in which cougars affected deer populations.

During the twentieth century, evidence showed that deer populations grew out of control in states where predators such as the cougar had been reduced or eliminated.

The first person to succeed in completing a serious field study was Maurice Hornocker, who began work in Montana and Idaho in the early 1960s. According to Hornocker, residents in Idaho "were convinced lions had killed all the deer and elk in Idaho and were eating each other."[28] Hornocker was determined to discover the truth. He and his associate, Wilbur Wiley, spent ten years tracking cougars through the rugged wilderness along the River of No Return in central Idaho.

Since there was no way of finding the elusive cougars and keeping them under constant surveillance, Hornocker had to resort to time-consuming and inefficient methods. He tracked the cougars with dogs, who treed the animals. Hornocker then used drugged darts to immobilize the big cats so that he could fix an ear tag on them. He and Wiley tracked the tagged animals and observed them as best they could but gained most of their information on movement, location, and numbers by continuing to capture the beasts and determining which had been tagged and where they had been last caught.

Using this method, Hornocker learned that cougars were highly territorial, particularly the males. His observations of the numbers of cougars and prey such as deer and elk revealed some startling conclusions. First, cougars were in serious trouble in the United States. Hornocker estimated their numbers at around sixty-five hundred and falling.

Second, he determined that cougar predation posed no threat to local deer and elk populations. Hornocker was the first to document evidence that, while deer and elk numbers in a particular area are most influenced by the availability of food, cougar population density has more to do with territoriality. He showed that cougars establish and maintain such large and exclusive territories that their population density will always be relatively sparse despite an abundance of prey. Because of this, there are never enough cougars in a particular location to seriously diminish the prey population. Animals such as deer, Hornocker discovered, reproduce quickly enough to easily replace losses to predation.

In fact, Hornocker and researchers who followed him found that cougars performed a useful service in maintaining healthy prey populations. One report cited by Ronald M. Nowak in *Walker's Mammals of the World* supported Hornocker, saying, "Deer and elk populations increased during [a] four-year study period, evidently being affected more by food availability than by cougar predation." But it went on to conclude that, "nonetheless, predation was thought to moderate prey oscillations, and to remove less fit individuals."[29] In other words, cougar predation, while posing no danger to deer and elk populations, kept the prey animal numbers from getting out of control and helped keep the general population healthy.

As a result of Hornocker's study, every state except Texas changed the status of the cougar from vermin to be shot on sight to a game animal subject to strict hunting regulations.

Radio collars

The most useful innovation in cougar research in the past half century has been the radio collar, developed by electronics experts with the help of biologist John Seidensticker in 1969. This device allowed researchers to replace the ear tags that revealed nothing about the cougar unless the animal was recaptured. The collars emit a radio signal that tells researchers exactly where the animal is at a given time.

Since cougars move too quickly through difficult terrain for humans to follow, the radio collars are of limited help in providing surveillance of the animals. But they can at least inform researchers of where a cougar has been. Researchers can then find cougar tracks and follow them either forward or backward to observe clues as to how the animal behaved. Tracks may lead a researcher to kills that show such things as what the cougar eats and how it gains its meals, travel patterns, and how often and where it rests. Researcher Ian Ross, who collected valuable information about cougars near the Sheep River in Alberta in the 1980s, said, "The key to our 13-year investigation of cougar ecology in Alberta has been the ability to find and follow the animal tracks."[30] This type of tracking is done most easily in snow, and so most fieldwork on cougars, including Ross's, has been done during the winter.

Radio collars are also useful in locating cougar dens. In addition, the collars alert researchers when the mother is

Researchers track a cougar's movement by means of the radio collar, a device that emits radio signals which reveal the animal's location.

Competition at the Top of the Food Chain

Radio-collar tracking of cougars revealed that the big cats are not always the aggressors in the natural world. Sometimes they find themselves under attack by rival predators. A five-year study conducted in the mid-1980s discovered that cougars often came out second best in encounters with grizzly bears or wolf packs. Sometimes the big cats were simply chased off; other times they were treed or even killed. Biologists documented two cases in which wolves killed cougars outright and seven other cases in which cougars died of starvation, "probably from getting bumped off kills by bears or wolves," according to John Wehausen, one of the University of California biologists who conducted the study.

In most of the United States, grizzly bears and wolves have fared even worse than cougars at the hands of humans. According to Wehausen, quoted by Martin Fortenzer in "Turf Wars at the Top of the Food Chain," in *Audubon* magazine, "In the absence of those predators, [mountain] lions are the top predators, and they're running the show."

The study is yet another demonstration of the ways that human interference has upset the balance of nature. Says Wehausen, "You start to realize how different things might have been in a lot of places when we had a full complement of predators."

Cougars are often outmatched when they encounter rival predators such as the grizzly bear.

away from her den, allowing them safe access to a close-up examination of the kittens. Taking advantage of this, Ian Ross learned facts about cougar litters that were in direct contradiction to accepted wisdom.

For example, most wild mammals in cold weather climates give birth in the spring, a survival strategy that has evolved so that babies can gain strength before they have to face the harsh winters. It was widely believed that this was true of cougars. But Ross reported, "At Sheep River, where winter weather can be severe, we have documented cougar litters born in every month of the year."[31] A good quarter of the cougar kittens were born between October and March.

Ross found that litters born in these bitter months were at least as likely to survive as those born in warmer weather. The kittens could withstand temperatures of minus 40 degrees Fahrenheit while the mother was away from the nest on hunting expeditions despite having virtually no shelter in their surface nests beyond a thin screen of vegetation.

Discovery of territorial conflict

A radio-collar study by Ken Logan and Linda Sweanor helped reveal some previously unsuspected aspects of cougar behavior. Over a ten-year period during the 1980s and '90s, Logan and Sweanor radio-tagged 241 cougars near the White Sands Missile Range in New Mexico.

They found that the big cats were not as respectful of other cougars' territory as was previously thought. In fact, their research revealed that territorial disputes between cougars were so common and fierce that they were the most frequent cause of death among the New Mexico cats. Logan and Sweanor also discovered that fights to the death occurred between males of neighboring territories and between resident males and immigrants trying to establish a territory of their own. As a result of these conflicts, territories were not permanent but constantly in a state of change.

The study also found that females did not defend their territory. Nonetheless, they, too, could fall victim to the larger, more aggressive males. Sometimes they were killed defending their kittens; sometimes fights broke out over rights to a kill. Occasionally, a hungry male would even kill a female for food.

The aggressiveness of the New Mexico males, which another study by Hornocker confirmed, showed that cougar behavior is more complex than previously thought and that their behavior can vary considerably from individual to individual and from one population to another.

DNA research

One of the most unlikely laboratories contributing to the study of cougars is at the National Cancer Institute in

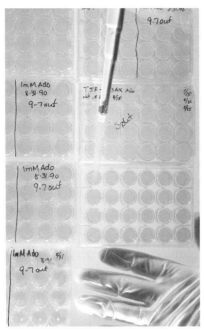

Scientists have found DNA analysis helpful in determining the relationships between animals.

Frederick, Maryland. Scientists at the institute's Laboratory of Genetic Diversity have been probing the possibility of using gene therapy, the manipulation of genetic material, as a way of treating or preventing cancer. In the process, they have developed skilled techniques of identifying, cataloging, and comparing DNA (deoxyribonucleic acid) in various animals, and determining the rate of DNA mutation.

Biologists have found this DNA information valuable in determining the relationships between animals. For example, DNA can determine whether minor physical differences in a population of cougars are significant enough to have the population declared a subspecies or whether they are simply within the range of individual variation expected in that group. DNA tests can help determine common ancestors of species and provide clues about the evolutionary pathways that modern species have followed.

It was the Laboratory of Genetic Diversity, with funding provided by the World Wildlife Fund, that helped biologists determine that a cougar recently found in New England was originally from Chile and therefore not a native animal and that cougars are actually the closest living relatives of the cheetah.

Obstacles in the way of research

In recent years, both government organizations and wildlife advocates have made efforts to fund cougar research. New Mexico gets high marks from many wildlife experts for its willingness to spend the money needed to gain accurate information about its cougars. In Brazil, Projeto Puma has been going on since 1988. The project is dedicated to the study of cougar-livestock interactions near human settlements in Brazil to determine the best ways of avoiding the kind of conflicts that lead to cries for the cougar's destruction.

However, these are exceptions to the rule. At present, the difficulty and great expense of studying cougars have prevented biologists from learning what they need to know about the animal in order to recommend wise game-management decisions.

Many obstacles stand in the way of a determined cougar researcher. Maurice Hornocker grew so frustrated over bureaucracy thwarting his research projects for the government that in 1984 he gave up and set up his own nonprofit research organization. He has had to scramble for funding ever since. Government rules continue to strangle needed research. Ironically, in their efforts to protect cougars in California, the Mountain Lion Foundation and its allies inadvertently blocked the state government from conducting cougar research. The state's Department of Fish and Game could fund research only on game animals; by passing the referendum banning the hunting of cougars, the voters removed cougars from the list of game animals that the department could study.

In some instances, taxpayers resent the huge expenses necessary to gain small amounts of information on cougars. One member of the Gila, New Mexico, Fish and Gun Club expressed the attitude of many when he said, "We probably spent four million dollars studying the mountain lion, and all we have proven is that it's a big pussycat and eats meat."[32]

Need for unbiased information

The scarcity of information has opened the door for heated arguments between opposing sides. There are still too few facts about cougars on which experts can agree. Even on such a basic matter as population numbers, experts argue over whether cougar numbers in certain areas are growing, declining, or stabilized. This has led to power struggles between those with opposing viewpoints, each of which focuses on scraps of research that appear to support its side.

In California, for example, those who oppose the ban on cougar hunting cite a recent study by the U.S. Forest Service. This report concludes that the protection of mountain lions in the state is responsible for increasing the cougar population to the point where it is hurting the deer population and becoming a growing menace to livestock producers. John Nicholson of California's Animal Damage Control says, "If the mountain lion density could be thinned in remote areas, the deer population could recover."[33]

Recent research indicates that a healthy population of predators can have a positive effect on its environment.

Those in favor of the hunting ban cite scientific reports such as Hornocker's showing that cougar densities have little effect on healthy deer populations. They accuse state game and fish departments of being tools of hunting organizations and are unwilling to give state wildlife officials the option of establishing a hunting season if they determine it is needed to control cougar populations.

As controversies become heated, both sides tend to simplify the issues to win approval for their arguments. If there is one thing wildlife researchers have found, however, it is that environmental issues are enormously complex. The effect of removing a seemingly insignificant animal from a habitat can be like removing a single card from a house of cards: The entire structure collapses. According to Bernhard Grzimek, recent research indicates that predators are more important than anyone ever imagined. A healthy predator population has been found to be one of the most reliable signs of a healthy habitat. Therefore, says Grzimek, "The intensified protection of carnivores is not any whim of nature lovers, but the surest way of safeguarding the future of large viable and life-preserving natural spaces, whose continued existence alone can make it possible for people to survive as well."[34]

The high stakes of the issue, as well as their complexity, guarantee that the only way controversies such as those that exist in California can be solved will be with solid research that clearly determines the status of cougars and their prey within a certain region.

6

Ensuring the Cougar's Survival

W ILDLIFE ADVOCATES WARN that even though cougar numbers have increased in the past few decades, their future remains precarious. Harold Danz believes that cougars have probably reached the peak of their recovery and now face a long, difficult battle for survival. Without concerned people making determined, intelligent efforts on behalf of cougars, they could end up as merely objects of curiosity confined to zoos.

Cougars could become objects of curiosity confined to zoos if people do not help them survive.

The hunting controversy

No cougar protection measures have generated as much passion and debate as antihunting ordinances. Hunting continues to be the leading known cause of individual cougar deaths, with an estimated twenty-five hundred killed in North America each year. Generally, in the words of wildlife writer Howard B. Quigley, "Sound management is replacing fear and indiscriminate hunting, although in some places the shift in human attitudes came too late."[35] There are still areas of South America, however, where hunting continues to pose a serious threat to the cougar's existence. Although most of these areas have laws regulating or banning cougar hunting, these laws are often poorly enforced. As a result, cougar populations are dwindling.

In the United States, the controversy over cougar hunting frequently divides two groups of people who are most interested in conservation: state game officials and wildlife advocates. Opponents of bans on cougar hunting argue that the bans have led to a dangerous overpopulation of cougars and give wildlife officials no means to correct the problem. Jim Haberstadt of the Oregon Fish and Game Commission called Measure 18, which banned hound hunting of cougars, "one of the most unfortunate incidents that has happened to wildlife management this century."[36]

Those in favor of allowing cougar hunts point to the animal's alarming population growth rate in California from two thousand in 1972 to an estimated six thousand in the late 1990s. Some Oregon officials at the state's Department of Fish and Wildlife warned that Oregon's cougar population has been experiencing a growth rate of between 4 and 5 percent annually. Hunting ban opponents note that the law does not prevent cougars from being killed; it just creates situations in which the animals cause destruction before they are killed and that Damage Control officials instead of hunters do the shooting. In 1995, for example, nearly twice as many cougars were killed by Damage Control officials in California than were killed by hunters in 1970, the last year hunting was allowed. They also argue that the unregulated growth of cougar populations is cruel to the animals because it forces some to survive in marginal or even suburban settings.

Hunting ban advocates counter by saying that hunting is not necessary to control cougar populations. They argue that the animal's recent population growth is merely a return to its former numbers and that the cougar's territorial nature will prevent the population from growing any further. According to the Predator Defense Institute of Eugene, Oregon, "In all the studies of [mountain] lions where relatively good documentation of lion numbers has been made, lion densities have peaked and stabilized at points between 10 and 20 square miles per adult resident."[37] Reputable biologists, including some within California's Department of Fish and Wildlife, say that the unhunted cougar population of California is, in fact, no longer growing—that it has stabilized over the past five years.

Reason, not emotion

Those who favor hunting bans are often suspicious of state game officials, whom they view as being controlled by hunting groups. The state of Texas, in particular, draws the ire of nature enthusiasts. "In Texas, you may kill as many mountain lions as you please, whenever you please," says Dede Armentrout of the National Audubon Society. The state justifies this by claiming that the cougar population is healthy and increasing despite the policy. But Armentrout counters, "We've lost a number of species over several decades because the Texas Parks and Wildlife Department didn't manage them. It kept saying, 'We've got plenty; don't worry your pretty little heads.'"[38]

Hunters, on the other hand, accuse wildlife advocates of being meddling do-gooders trying to impose their narrow beliefs on everyone else. This antagonistic state of affairs has led to concerns that the management of cougars has degenerated into a political battle with each side using its own statistics to back up its arguments, rather than a rational, unbiased look at the scientific data.

Harold Danz argues that a comprehensive approach to managing wildlife populations can provide the best conditions for cougar survival. He notes that where officials actively manage game such as elk and deer, these populations

Environmental and conservation groups have helped raise awareness of the plight of the Florida panther.

are thriving. Danz believes that this comprehensive management can best be achieved if states are allowed the option of using hunting to control local cougar populations.

In the 1990s, Montana's Department of Fish, Wildlife, and Parks provided a model of how objective evaluation of scientific data can be used to decide cougar-hunting issues. Officials from the department originally proposed to allow the sport-hunting of cougars in Paradise Valley, with a limit of five cougars per season. However, after research indicated that such hunting would probably result in the eventual extermination of the small Paradise Valley cougar population, officials withdrew the hunting proposal.

Changing attitudes

The work of a wide variety of environmental and conservation groups such as the Mountain Lion Foundation, the Predator Defense Institute, and the Predator Conservation Alliance has made considerable headway in changing Americans' attitudes about the cougar. Whereas a century ago, most people viewed cougars as a menace to be wiped out wherever possible, now a vast majority favor taking steps to protect the animals.

This is especially true in areas such as Florida, where cougars are fighting for their survival. A survey of state residents in the late 1990s showed that 58 percent were aware that the Florida panther was endangered, and more than nine in ten supported actions to save the animal from extinction. In a huge turnabout from former times, 87 percent disagreed that a thriving panther population posed a threat to the state's economic prosperity. In fact, 83 percent of Floridians favored attempts to import cougars to reinvigorate the dying local population.

A similar trend in favor of cougar preservation has been taking place even in western areas where cougars are not presently endangered. A recent survey of residents in Colorado's Rocky Mountains found that an overwhelming 80 percent believed that restrictions should be placed on human development in areas with cougar populations.

"There's a value shift about how people view wildlife," concludes Michael Manfredo, a professor at Colorado State University. This includes "a high willingness to accept mountain lions on the urban fringe—even if they kill people."[39]

Wildlife groups continue to reach out to the public with educational programs and campaigns to make people aware of the challenges that wildlife face in the modern world, and the consequences of ignoring their plight.

Habitat preservation

Even strong public sympathy for wildlife can quickly melt away when animal protection measures threaten personal lifestyle and economic choices. Historically, the greatest opposition to cougars has been from those who suffered the greatest economic loss because of cougars, generally livestock loss. Similarly, support for cougars is likely to evaporate if it means imposing tight restrictions on where people live or causes a drop in their standard of living. It has been a long-term trend that, as long as the human population increases, it will take over resources that once served wildlife, and all other species will decline. That is why wildlife supporters advocate population-control education as the only long-term means of ensuring habitat survival.

Cougar attacks on livestock (pictured) enrage livestock owners, whose personal lifestyle and economic choices are jeopardized by the attacks.

A related habitat concern is that developing of wilderness into land more economically useful to humans has historically been associated with progress. The twin goals of economic progress and wilderness preservation are in many ways directly opposed. This makes solutions difficult to find.

Some people, such as Harold Danz, believe the answer to habitat preservation is setting aside government-owned lands that are free from development:

> The establishment of continued support for government enclaves such as parks, forests and wildlife sanctuaries, coupled with the unsuitability of certain large public tracts of western land for expanding human use, should permit the cougar to continue to thrive and its population further increase.[40]

This optimism, however, runs into the problem of fragmentation. Cougars need huge expanses of continuous habitat. A patchwork of wildlife refuges throughout the country will only succeed in isolating cougar populations from each other, where they will wither away like the Florida panther.

Biologist Paul Beier notes that, for the wildlife preserve system to work, it will have to include forest corridors between wilderness areas to prevent populations from being isolated. Wildlife advocates in California have been working hard to make this a reality by placing Propositions 12 and 13 on the state ballot. These propositions would allow the state to issue bonds to raise money for habitat protection, including $82.5 million for the establishment of wildlife corridors.

The most ambitious proposal by wildlife advocates for carrying out the corridor concept is the "Paseo Pantera." This would be a system of parks and wilderness areas connected by corridors that would form a continuous path all the way from southern Argentina and Chile to British Columbia. Although such a proposal offers the greatest hope for wildlife survival, it faces enormous political obstacles, not the least of which is that it would require close cooperation among dozens of governments.

On a smaller scale, biologists suggest that building underpasses where highways cut through wilderness habitat would keep roads from forming deadly barriers to wildlife movement. Florida has already paid a considerable price to put this suggestion into practice. It has built thirty-six highway underpasses along the interstate highways that cut through Florida panther habitat, at a cost of nearly $1 million each. The Predator Conservation Alliance is also lobbying the government to curtail the building of roads in national forests, to close many of the roads now in existence, and to ban all off-road vehicle use in these forests.

Genetic restoration

Vanishing local populations and subspecies such as the Florida panther present a special challenge to biologists intent on their preservation. Wildlife managers can take positive steps

such as preserving the present habitat, fostering an increase in the number of cougar prey such as deer, and tightening regulations to eliminate mercury poisoning. But even with the best management, scientists agree that the Florida panther population is too small and genetically inbred to survive for long.

Scientists agree that even with the best management, the Florida panther population is too small and genetically inbred to survive for long.

Biologists have tried to solve this problem by cross-breeding the Florida panthers with cougars from other locations. They have tried captive breeding, taking panthers from the wild and breeding them with other cougars, and have relocated western panthers to Florida.

Wildlife managers began the relocation program in 1988, when they released and tracked seven Texas cougars into northern Florida to see if they could survive in that part of the state. The experiment did not work. Three of the seven died within a year of their release. The others began establishing themselves too close to urban centers and were sent back to Texas.

From 1993 to 1995, biologists brought Texas cougars back into Florida. Again, the cats were frequently spotted too close to civilization and were removed. The program finally achieved some success in 1995 when a group of eight Texas females were released into Florida panther habitat. By the end of 1996, scientists counted four litters of Texas-Florida hybrids.

Biologists are now certain that they can introduce Texas cougars into the Florida panther population to provide desperately needed genetic diversity. Some wildlife experts question whether this is a good thing. They note that by mixing Texas cougars into the population, the Florida subspecies is being bred out of existence. Scientists, however, say that at this late stage they have no choice: The pure Florida subspecies is already doomed, and if there are to be any cougars in Florida, the Florida panthers will have to interbreed with western cougars.

Reducing human-cougar conflict

By their nature, cougars will always have the potential to create danger and economic problems whenever their habitat conflicts with that of humans. Paul Beier says, "It is impossible to reduce this small risk to zero without eliminating either cougars or humans from cougar habitat. Neither is acceptable."[41]

Humans have zero tolerance for cougars within urban or suburban areas, and any cougar living on the edge of such areas does so at its peril. Harold Danz is adamant that any cougars living near human developments, even though they are in traditional cougar habitat, must be removed. Any increase in the number of cougar attacks on humans is likely to fuel calls for hunting or removing the animals.

As long as cougars make use of their masterful ability to hide and remain mysterious creatures of the woods, they are generally safe. But as Dave Fjelline of the California Animal Damage Control observes, "When [mountain] lion sighting becomes common, trouble often follows."[42] The cougar is a highly adaptable creature and, to survive, could adapt itself to staying out of sight in such settings. Aggressive or careless cougars may eventually be eliminated by predator control, leaving only the secretive, the stealthy, and the wary.

Experts suggest that people living at the edge of cougar habitat adopt a strategy similar to that of the early pioneers. They should alter the land immediately surrounding the human living areas so that it is inhospitable to cougars. "The key to preventing or reducing cougar encounters in urban areas lies in modifying habitat to be less attractive to prey species,"[43] advises the Predator Defense Institute. Installation of outdoor lighting discourages cougars from approaching, as does the elimination of dense ground cover in which cougars can hide while stalking prey.

Livestock losses

One area in which the colonial prejudices and tactics against predators are still in effect is livestock loss. The Predator Conservation Alliance claims,

> The U.S. Department of Agriculture's "Wildlife Services" program is perhaps the worst example of outdated and misguided government policy toward predator conflict resolution. Most Americans have no idea that more than $36 million of their taxes are spent annually by this federal program to kill nearly 100,000 predators—coyotes, black bears, mountain lions, foxes, and wolves—each year in 17 western states.[44]

Once endangered, the bison recovered because concerned individuals took actions on its behalf. The same kind of effort is now needed to protect the cougar from extinction.

The Predator Conservation Alliance is pushing hard to eliminate this program and replace it with regulations requiring nonlethal control methods to be tried first. Harold Danz suggests that cougar attacks on livestock could be reduced by removing livestock from cougar habitat. He notes that the government is actually financing cougar-livestock conflict by compensating ranchers for livestock killed by cougars. Danz proposes ending these payments, thereby discouraging ranchers from running their operations near cougar territory. Such a program, however, would require the strict enforcement of laws protecting the cougar, as Brazil has discovered. Although the cougar is protected by law in that country and no compensation is made for livestock losses, poor law enforcement has resulted in ranchers and farmers ignoring the laws and killing cougars on their own.

Concerned individuals

Because humans have so destroyed the ecological balance of nature, most other large animal species on earth are unable to defend themselves from the encroachments of civilization. Those endangered species that have made recoveries in the past, such as the bison, have done so because concerned individuals took actions on their behalf. The same is likely true for the cougar.

These efforts may be on a small scale, such as Michael Jurich's Prairie View Wind Wild Animal Refuge. This one-man operation provides a private refuge for nine cougars in a remote area of Colorado. More commonly, concerned individuals join together to form groups such as the Mountain Lion Foundation or the Predator Conservation Alliance. Their determination will go a long way in deciding whether, generations from now, the only remaining cougars are confined to zoos and small, controlled wildlife enclosures, or whether the ghost of the mountains still runs free.

Notes

Introduction

1. Quoted in Jerry Kobalenko, *Forest Cats of North America*. Buffalo, NY: Firefly, 1997, p. 8.

2. Quoted in Harold P. Danz, *Cougar!* Athens, OH: Swallow Press, 1999, p. xiii.

3. Quoted in "Lions on the Hunt," *Outdoor Life*, January 1996, p. 14.

Chapter 1: Decline of the Cougar

4. Quoted in Kobalenko, *Forest Cats of North America*, p. 38.

5. Quoted in Predator Defense Institute, www.enviroweb.org/pdi/index.html.

6. Quoted in "Lions on the Hunt," p. 16.

7. Quoted in "Lions on the Hunt," p. 14.

8. Quoted in Harry Thurston, "Can the Eastern Cougar Debate Be Laid to Rest?" *Canadian Geographic*, September 1999, p. 18.

Chapter 2: Life of a Wild Cougar

9. Quoted in Kobalenko, *Forest Cats of North America*, p. 11.

10. Danz, *Cougar!* p. 31.

Chapter 3: Cougars Versus Humans: Hunting

11. Bernhard Grzimek, *Grzimek's Encyclopedia of Mammals*, vol. 3. New York: McGraw-Hill, 1990, p. 369.

12. Ted Williams, "The Lion's Silent Return," *Audubon*, November 1994, p. 29.

13. Quoted in Kobalenko, *Forest Cats of North America*, p. 80.

14. Danz, *Cougar!* p. 60.

Chapter 4: Cougars Versus Humans: Habitat Loss

15. Grzimek, *Grzimek's Encyclopedia of Mammals*, vol. 3, p. 370.

16. Danz, *Cougar!* p. 210.

17. Quoted in Danz, *Cougar!* p. 110.

18. Williams, "The Lion's Silent Return," p. 84.

19. Quoted in Susan Zakin, "Looking for Bighorns in All the Wrong Places?" *Field & Stream,* January 1999, p. 20.

20. Quoted in Marc Peyser, "Predators on the Prowl," *Newsweek*, January 8, 1996, p. 58.

21. "Cat in the Ballot Box," *Field & Stream*, March 1996, p. 30.

22. Williams, "The Lion's Silent Return," p. 34.

23. Melody E. Roelke et al., "Mercury Contamination in Florida Panthers," Florida Panther Society, www.atlantic.net/~oldfla/panther/pather.html.

Chapter 5: Trying to Understand Cougars

24. Quoted in Predator Defense Institute website.

25. Kevin Hansen, *Cougar: The American Lion.* Flagstaff, AZ: Northland Publishers, 1992, p. xiii.

26. Quoted in Howard B. Quigley, "Encounters with a Silent Predator," *Natural History*, December 1994, p. 57.

27. Quoted in Danz, *Cougar!* p. 138.

28. Quoted in Williams, "The Lion's Silent Return," p. 30.

29. Ronald M. Nowak, *Walker's Mammals of the World*, vol. 2, 5th ed. Baltimore, MD: Johns Hopkins University Press, 1991, p. 1205.

30. Ian Ross, "Lions in Winter," *Natural History*, December 1994, p. 52.

31. Ross, "Lions in Winter," p. 52.

32. Quoted in Williams, "The Lion's Silent Return," p. 30.

33. Quoted in "Cat in the Ballot Box," p. 30.

34. Grzimek, *Grzimek's Encyclopedia of Mammals*, vol. 3, p. 370.

Chapter 6: Ensuring the Cougar's Survival

35. Quigley, "Encounters with a Silent Predator," p. 57.

36. Quoted in Predator Defense Institute website.

37. Predator Defense Institute website.

38. Quoted in Williams, "The Lion's Silent Return," p. 32.

39. Quoted in Peyser, "Predators on the Prowl," p. 58.

40. Danz, *Cougar!* p. 156.

41. Quoted in Kobalenko, *Forest Cats of North America*, p. 87.

42. Quoted in "Cat in the Ballot Box," p. 30.

43. Predator Defense Institute website.

44. Predator Conservation Alliance, www.predator conservation.org.

Organizations to Contact

American Zoo and Aquarium Association (AZA)
8403 Colesville Rd., Suite 710
Silver Spring, MD 20910
(301) 562-0888 • fax: (301) 907-2980
website: www.aza.org • e-mail: membership@aza.org

AZA represents over 160 zoos and aquariums in North America. The association provides information on captive breeding of endangered species, conservation education, natural history, and wildlife legislation. AZA publications include conservation and science publications, the *AZA Annual Report*, and *Communique,* a monthly magazine. Publications are available from the Publications Department at the address listed above.

Endangered Species Coalition (ESC)
1101 14th St. NW, Suite 1200
Washington, DC 20003
(202) 682-9400 • fax: (202) 682-1331
website: www.stopextinction.org • e-mail: esc@stopextinction.org

The coalition is composed of conservation, professional, and animal welfare groups that work to extend the Endangered Species Act and to ensure its enforcement. ESC encourages public activism through grassroots organizations, direct lobbying, and letter-writing and telephone campaigns. Its publications include the book *The Endangered Species Act: A Commitment Worth Keeping*, and articles, fact sheets, position papers, and bill summaries regarding the Endangered Species Act.

The Florida Panther Society

Route 1, Box 1895
White Springs, Florida 32096
(904) 397-2945
website: www.atlantic.net/~oldfla/panther/panther.html

A non-profit environmental and support organization dedicated to the recovery of the Florida Panther. Through re-introduction, genetic restoration, and habitat preservation, it hopes to help the Florida panther make a recovery. It encourages people to express their concerns about the plight of the Florida panther to Florida legislators.

Foundation for Research on Economics and the Environment (FREE)

945 Technology Blvd., Suite 101F
Bozeman, MT 59718
(406) 585-1776 • fax: (406) 585-3000
website: www.free-eco.org • e-mail: free@mcn.net

FREE is a research and education foundation committed to freedom, environmental quality, and economic progress. The foundation works to reform environmental policy by using the principles of private property rights, the free market, and the rule of law. FREE publishes the quarterly newsletter *FREE Perspectives on Economics and the Environment,* and produces a biweekly syndicated op-ed column.

Hornocker Wildlife Institute

PO Box 3246
University of Idaho
Moscow, ID 83845
(208) 885-6871 • fax: (208) 885-2999
website: www.hwi.org • e-mail: hwi@hwi.org

Founded by Dr. Maurice Hornocker, the Hornocker Wildlife Institute conducts long-term research on threatened species and sensitive ecological systems. Through observation and exploration a framework is provided for satisfying a universal curiosity about the nature of wildlife and the effects of humans on the natural environment. The institute is a world leader in carnivore research and continues to work on these important indicators of ecological health. It is also broadening its focus through ongoing studies of whooping cranes and trumpeter swans, steelhead and salmon, wilderness vegetation succession, and wildlife populations in Latin America. In addition, it continues to press ahead in integrating good science and broad-based ecosystem approaches with cultural and economic factors.

IUCN/SSC Cat Specialist Group
Attn: Peter Jackson, Chairman
1172 Bougy
Switzerland
+41-21-808-6012
website: http://lynx.uio.no/catfolk • e-mail: pjackson@iprolink.ch

The Cat Specialist Group is an international panel of over 170 scientists, wildlife managers, and other specialists from forty countries who have volunteered their expertise to the Species Survival Commission of IUCN—the World Conservation Union, which is based in Switzerland. Its function is to provide IUCN, CITES (Convention on International Trade in Endangered Species), and governmental and nongovernmental organizations with advice on all matters concerning wild cats, including their status in nature, the threats they face, conservation requirements, and biology and natural history. The group publishes the newsletter *Cat News* to its members.

National Wildlife Federation (NWF)
8925 Leesburg Pike
Vienna, VA 22184
(703) 790-4000
website: www.nwf.org

The National Wildlife Federation offers environmental education programs in communities, in the outdoors, and in the classroom. Publications include: *National Wildlife* and *International Wildlife*, bimonthly magazines serving to educate readers about national and global conservation issues; *Ecodemia*, a book regarding campus environmental stewardship at the turn of the twenty-first century; *Conservation Directory*, featuring descriptions and contact information for over three thousand environmental organizations and government agencies; and *NWF Special Reports*, which are on-line environmental reports.

PERC
502 South 19th Ave.
Bozeman, MT 59715
(406) 587-9591 • fax: (406) 586-7555
website: www.perc.org • e-mail: perc@perc.org

PERC (The Political Economy Research Center) is a nationally recognized institute located in Bozeman, Montana. The primary goal is to provide market solutions to environmental problems. PERC pioneered the approach known as free market environmentalism. It is based on the following tenets: Private property rights encourage stewardship of resources; government subsidies often degrade the environment; market incentives spur individuals to conserve resources and protect environmental quality; polluters should be liable for the harm they cause others. Activities include research and policy analysis, outreach through conferences, books and articles, and environmental education at all levels. Publications include the quarterly newsletter *PERC Reports*, books by PERC authors and editors, and the Policy Series featuring short papers that apply the principles of property rights and markets to natural resource issues.

Predator Conservation Alliance
PO Box 6733
Bozeman, MT 59771
(406) 587-3389
www.predatorconservation.org

The Predator Conservation Alliance has been working since 1991 to conserve, protect, and restore native predators, primarily those, such as the cougar, that live in the Northern Rockies and High Plains.

United Nations Environment Programme (UNEP)
Attn: Mr. Tore J. Brevik, Chief of Information and Public Affairs
PO Box 30552
Nairobi, Kenya
+254-2-62-1234/3292 • fax: +254-2-62-3927/3692
website: www.unep.ch • e-mail: ipainfo@unep.org

UNEP studies ecosystems, encourages environmental management and planning, and helps developing countries deal with their environmental problems. UNEP's publications include environmental briefs, the bimonthly magazine *Our Planet*, and numerous books available through its publications catalogue.

U.S. Fish and Wildlife Service
1849 C St. NW
Washington, DC 20240
(202) 208-3100
website: www.fws.gov • e-mail: web_reply@fws.gov

The U.S. Fish and Wildlife Service is a network of regional offices, national wildlife refuges, research and development centers, national fish hatcheries, and wildlife law enforcement agencies. The service's primary goal is to conserve, protect, and enhance fish and wildlife and their habitats. It publishes an endangered species list as well as fact sheets, pamphlets, and information on the Endangered Species Act.

World Wildlife Fund (WWF)
1250 24th St. NW
PO Box 97180
Washington, DC 20077-7180
(800) CALL-WWF
website: www.worldwildlife.org

WWF is dedicated to protecting the world's wildlife and wildlands. The largest privately supported international conservation organization in the world, WWF directs its conservation efforts toward three global goals: protecting endangered spaces, saving endangered species, and addressing global threats. From working to save the giant panda, tiger, and rhino to helping establish and manage parks and reserves worldwide, WWF has been a conservation leader for more than thirty-eight years. WWF publishes an endangered species list, the bimonthly newsletter *Focus*, and a variety of books on the environment.

Suggestions for Further Reading

Jerry Kobalenko, *Forest Cats of North America*. Buffalo, NY: Firefly, 1997. This is one of those rare adult books that presents scientific and natural history information in a style that is exciting and readable enough for young readers; includes good use of photographs.

"Lions on the Hunt," *Outdoor Life*, January 1996.

Marc Peyser, "Predators on the Prowl," *Newsweek*, January 8, 1996.

Works Consulted

Books

Harold P. Danz, *Cougar!* Athens, OH: Swallow Press, 1999. A thorough documentation of cougar issues, in which the author offers his own, sometimes controversial, suggestions for dealing with them.

Bernhard Grzimek, *Grzimek's Encyclopedia of Mammals.* Vol. 3. New York: McGraw-Hill, 1990. An encyclopedia that provides unusual detail and opinion on wildlife concerns.

Kevin Hansen, *Cougar: The American Lion.* Flagstaff, AZ: Northland Publishers, 1992. This book, sponsored by the Mountain Lion Foundation, brings a wealth of information as well as a cougar advocate's point of view.

Ronald M. Nowak, *Walker's Mammals of the World.* Vol. 2, 5th ed. Baltimore, MD: Johns Hopkins University Press, 1991. Fairly standard encyclopedia format.

Periodicals

"Cat in the Ballot Box," *Field & Stream*, March 1996.

"Lions on the Hunt," *Outdoor Life*, January 1996.

Martin Fortenzer, "Turf Wars at the Top of the Food Chain," *Audubon*, November 1997.

Marc Peyser, "Predators on the Prowl," *Newsweek*, January 8, 1996.

Howard B. Quigley, "Encounters with a Silent Predator," *Natural History*, December 1994.

Ian Ross, "Lions in Winter," *Natural History*, December

1994.

Harry Thurston, "Can the Eastern Cougar Debate Be Laid to Rest?" *Canadian Geographic*, September 1999.

Ted Williams, "The Lion's Silent Return," *Audubon*, November 1994.

Susan Zakin, "Looking for Bighorns in All the Wrong Places?" *Field & Stream,* January 1999.

Websites

Predator Conservation Alliance, www.predatorconservation.org.

Predator Defense Institute,www.enviroweb.org/pdi/index.html.

Melody E. Roelke et al., "Mercury Contamination in Florida Panthers," Florida Panther Society, www.atlantic.net/~oldfla/panther/panther.html.

Index

Picture Credits

About the Author

Nathan Aaseng is the author of more than 150 books for young readers on a variety of subjects. His interest in the topic of cougars is inspired by one of his son's total fascination with wild animals. Aaseng, from Eau Claire, Wisconsin, was the 1999 recipient of the Wisconsin Library Association's Notable Wisconsin Author Award.